HOUSING POLICY TRANSFORMED

The right to buy and the desire to own

Peter King

This edition published in Great Britain in 2010 by

The Policy Press
University of Bristol
Fourth Floor
Beacon House
Queen's Road
Bristol BS8 1QU
UK

Tel +44 (0)117 331 4054
Fax +44 (0)117 331 4093
e-mail tpp-info@bristol.ac.uk
www.policypress.org.uk

North American office:
The Policy Press
c/o International Specialized Books Services (ISBS)
920 NE 58th Avenue, Suite 300
Portland, OR 97213-3786, USA
Tel +1 503 287 3093
Fax +1 503 280 8832
e-mail info@isbs.com

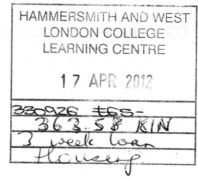

British Library Cataloguing in Publication Data
A catalogue record for this book is available from the British Library.

Library of Congress Cataloging-in-Publication Data
A catalog record for this book has been requested.

ISBN 978 1 84742 213 2 hardcover

Cover design by The Policy Press
Front cover: image kindly supplied by www.istock.com
Printed and bound in Great Britain by TJ International, Padstow

To all my friends at the IEA

Contents

Preface

When I first had the idea for this book in 2006 I saw the project as being predominantly historical, with it concentrating on what the Right to Buy (RTB) achieved and the criticisms against it. My aim was to locate the RTB into current (that is, 2006) thinking on owner occupation in Britain. This was at a time of rapidly increasing house prices and a growing concern about affordability. My idea was to compare the RTB with more recent initiatives aimed at promoting owner occupation and dealing with access to the tenure, particularly for those on low incomes. I also wanted to say something about the status of social housing as a subsidiary tenure now used by the government to support the majority tenure. I have kept partially to this original intention, but the collapse of the housing market since 2007 has led me to shift the focus of the book somewhat. The recession in the housing market, and the economy generally, has changed the context of the debate about the RTB and meant that the focus of this book has also had to alter. My view of the criticisms of the RTB had been that they were largely historical and that the critics *had lost*. After all, the RTB was about to celebrate its 30th anniversary with absolutely no prospect of it being repealed. One could therefore afford to be charitable with the RTB's critics because they were no longer of any real significance. But this has now changed and the RTB has again been challenged and there have been calls for it to be suspended or even abolished. Perhaps of more significance is the fact that 2008 saw a massive decline in sales due to the state of the housing market.

Of particular importance, it seems to me, is the role played in the current financial crisis by the promotion by the government of low-income owner occupation. The link to the collapse of the sub-prime housing market in the US has been clearly established (Shiller, 2008) and this can be seen as part of a deliberate push by US governments from President Carter onwards to promote owner occupation to hitherto excluded groups (Ferguson, 2008; Butler, 2009). Whilst the government cannot be held responsible for the development of the derivatives market built on mortgage lending, we might suggest that its promotion of owner occupation to low-income households has assisted in creating this unpredictable flow of highly toxic debt.

Governments in the UK have been equally intent on extending owner occupation to low-income households. This was seen most recently with the Labour government's housing Green Paper in 2007 (CLG, 2007) with its ambitious building targets and promotion of pathways to ownership. But, of course, the most significant attempt by a British government to promote low-income owner occupation was also one of the earliest, namely, the RTB.

It is now clear that these policies promoting owner occupation have had unintended consequences, and so it is opportune to explore the most important and iconic of these in this new light. In particular, we can question whether governments have a duty to promote the desire to own property, and, if they do, how this matches up with their other responsibilities such as meeting unmet housing need. We need to understand why the government did such a thing as the RTB.

In response to the changes in the economic and political climate I have chosen not to engage in any great detail with what might be called the traditional arguments on the RTB. Of course, I mention these, but they do not now make up a particularly large part of my discussion. These arguments have been rehearsed on many occasions and, as I have stated, the battle has been fought and won by the RTB. The RTB is still here, being taken up by social tenants, albeit in very much smaller numbers and with less generous support. But the debate has moved on and the RTB is now facing a different challenge, not from those who seek to defend social housing, but rather from those who take a less tenure-bound view of housing and look at the issues from the effect they have on individual households. The debate is now best seen as being *post-RTB*, or more generally post-owner-occupation. It is a debate that could only take place because the RTB and the desire to own had won politically. The argument now is what we do when some can have their desire fulfilled – and with the aid of the state – whilst others cannot.

As I discuss in Chapter 5, we might see these new criticisms of the RTB, based around the collapse of housing markets, as opportunistic, in the sense that it might just be the old critics merely using the cloak of a recession to justify their antipathy. There may indeed be some of this, but we should not lose sight of the fact that the criticism of the RTB has been generated not because of the problems with social housing, but because of those with owner occupation. It is, therefore, a very different debate that we now face and, whether critics are being opportunistic or not, we still have to listen to what they are actually saying and respond accordingly. What matters now is how the RTB could be justified.

This change in the economic and political climate, however, does not alter the overall view I have of the RTB and its significance. In particular, I need to make a clear distinction between the RTB and later policies introduced by governments in the UK and the US. The RTB cannot be implicated in the causes of the financial crisis. The RTB has existed through two recessions as well as extended periods of economic growth, and this suggests that it might provide some lessons about how to encourage low-cost owner occupation in a sustainable way. The RTB, whatever one may think of it, succeeded in what it set out to do, and understanding what those aims were and why they succeeded is what this book seeks to achieve.

But the RTB remains controversial, and doubtless always will. What is not possible, unfortunately, is reaching a settled view where supporters and critics of the RTB are reconciled. Of course, at the political level there is a clear consensus, with no really serious political threat to the RTB in the future, despite the new wave of criticism it has faced since 2008. But in academic and professional circles there is still a tremendous hostility with occasional islands of support amongst mavericks and in certain think tanks. What does not exist is any compatibility between the political support for the policy and the academic and professional antipathy. So, in writing about the RTB, should we even seek to reconcile these two views?

We might see this as important in that any critic of the RTB will most likely see this book as unbalanced precisely because it does not take a wholly critical approach. The antipathy towards the RTB is so ingrained, so taken for granted, that any attempt at a different approach will automatically be seen as partial at best and as an ill-considered rant at worst. This being so, should we not strive for a complete view? Of course, we might not be able to agree over what is 'complete': for some this might simply be taken to mean 'completely critical'. However, as I have just stated, what I mean is a reconciliation of all possible views.

Having spent some time considering the possibility of reconciliation I have come to the conclusion that it is not possible, and perhaps not desirable. It is not desirable because I see no reason to give my opponents any unnecessary succour and support. If I am going to be criticised for the positions I have taken why should I help others to re-arm and get their position across? After all, it is my view that has seldom been heard and critics of the RTB have had a pretty much open field. Stating my position boldly, why should I present the arguments that have already been well aired at the expense of ideas and positions that are seldom, if ever, heard?

In any case, seeking reconciliation is a difficult and sometimes fruitless task. In January 2009 Israel invaded the Gaza Strip in an attempt to deal with the threat of Hamas. Here we have two sides of a long-standing argument – Israelis and Palestinians – who stand implacably opposed to each other, both seeing themselves as defending 'their' land against those intent on taking it. Both sides can call on a holy book for support and both have their military suppliers to help them give action to their offence. Sharing the land they fight over seems to be impossible and so they fight and kill each other. Without wishing to be overblown, we can see the debate over the RTB in similar terms, if as farce rather than as tragedy. Here we have two opposing visions of housing, one based on individual freedom and personal responsibility and the other on solidarity and social need. Neither side can see the position of the other and nor are they prepared to admit that their opponent's case has any merit. Under the slightest taunt either side will resort to their fallback positions and marshal their criticisms and insults, whilst blaming the other side for their intemperance. Both sides are too busy being right and being angry to listen to what the other is saying.

Of course, with the RTB, the stakes are rather low and we should not overuse the analogy with real life-and-death conflicts. Indeed, we might say that the real horror of life in Gaza, with the loss of life and lack of reason, shows just how petty and insignificant our academic debates actually are. We perhaps need to remember that unnecessary arguments are usually referred to as 'academic'. What we are arguing over when we discuss the RTB is not life and death, it is not about existential threats, but about how we might, amidst our general affluence, stability and calm, live a little better. No one is really a loser in the manner we see on our television screens. Perhaps we ought to bear this in mind the next time we debate housing policy in the UK. We do tend to dramatise our problems and we should be aware of this and try to restrain ourselves a bit. In the more than 25 years I have been involved with housing policy and practice there has always been talk of a housing crisis in Britain. No matter how much money is spent, how many new dwellings are built and whatever new policies are enacted, there is always a crisis.

But this continued overuse of the word 'crisis' cheapens the concept: we ought to reserve this word for things like the destruction of houses in Gaza city, or the aftermath of floods and earthquakes (both of which happened with disastrous effects in 2008), or for the situation in Darfur with millions living in insanitary conditions under constant threat of attack. Despite our pretentions towards science, we academics are not really very good at keeping things in proportion and adopting a properly relative position. We should, of course, be concerned with housing conditions in the UK and with those who cannot help themselves. We should as a society be seeking to better our lot and ensure we live as well as possible. It is largely for these reasons that we elect politicians and agree to pay our taxes. But we do need to maintain a sense of proportion and see how we can and do live relative to others before we claim there is a crisis, and this applies especially when we are seeking to create and sustain change within our own society. When we refer to crises in housing policy and refer to policies such as the RTB as a disaster, we should remember what is actually going on in Darfur, Zimbabwe or Gaza, and I say this not out of any sense of piety or priggishness, and certainly not as a means of slipping out of any debate about housing policy in the UK, but rather to retain some sense of perspective about what we are really arguing about and what it actually means.

This is, undoubtedly, an argument that works both ways, and so we need to be very careful about making any significant claims about housing policies such as the RTB. We should avoid positive hyperbole as much as the negative variety. We should be careful when we claim a policy has been successful or that it has transformed society. Accordingly, I try to be very careful in what I claim for the RTB and to make sure I can back it up.

More generally we need to remember that no policy, however brilliant or tuned in to the popular feeling of the day, can prevent the unexpected, or ward off the genuine disaster. Policy making operates only within rather safe and predictable margins (and this applies even if we accept that we do not fully understand these parameters and cannot claim we are prepared for all situations [King, 2009]). Once we enter the realm of uncertainty the sorts of policies we are discussing here are not particularly useful or even that relevant. Policies like the RTB can only be successful because we exist with reasonably secure and safe parameters. We operate within a system that only seldom experiences sudden shocks or disasters. It is a system with considerable margins of safety built in as a result of affluence and the political settlement that underpins it. We have to lose a considerable amount before we face a genuine existential threat, and this applies even to the situation of 2008/09 where house prices are falling and repossessions increasing (before you try to disagree, remember Darfur!). We may not be very well prepared to face threats to our comfort and security, and we may magnify those which we do face out of naivety or ignorance, but still we exist with a stable political culture. Indeed, it is this very stability that allows us to argue over matters of tenure rather than figuring out the best way to avoid the rockets and raiding militias.

Acknowledgements

I have several people to thank for their help and support whilst I have been writing this book. My colleagues at the Centre for Comparative Housing Research, Tim Brown and Mike Oxley, have commented on various parts of this book and offered challenging and useful insights, which made me question some of my arguments, explain some better and drop others that did not work as well as I thought they did.

Over recent years I have received much inspiration from my contact with the Institute of Economic Affairs. The IEA remains the ideal type for a think tank – honest, intellectually rigorous and always questioning – and it is always a pleasure to visit 2 Lord North Street. I have had the pleasure of discussing the RTB with the IEA's former director, John Blundell, who has also very kindly read the book in manuscript form. I also need to thank the regular contributors to the IEA's blog, where I have been able to post some of my thoughts on housing and the RTB in particular. I am grateful to Richard Wellings and his colleagues who have established such a stimulating forum for ideas.

My thanks also go to staff at The Policy Press: first, to Karen Bowler for taking the risk of accepting this book and for encouraging me to be controversial and develop the book as I wished, and, second, to Emily Watt for her support and helpfulness throughout the process. I am also grateful to the anonymous reviewers who have commented on this proposal at various stages.

There are certain people, or perhaps, rather, types of people, who I had in mind when writing this book. I have imagined how they would react to my arguments, and if I felt they would disagree or find them outrageous then I had felt that I am on the right lines. There is a childish aspect to this, but it has allowed me to clarify my intention of putting together a book that looks at the RTB differently.

As always my family bear the brunt of the solitary and selfish process of writing. They have listened to me, responded to my questions and anxieties, helped to choose the cover and, most importantly, provided the necessary relief from writing. The kindness and concern of those I can rely on is always a comfort, and so I thank B, Helen and Rachel.

ONE

Introduction

So many initiatives in housing are announced with a huge fanfare, as if they will solve the 'housing problem' and transform housing structures. New policies are described as the ones that create lasting and permanent change. Since the late 1980s we can point to any number of new initiatives such as Tenants' Choice, Housing Action Trusts, Housing Investment Trusts, private finance and stock transfer, all aimed at altering the structure of housing provision by introducing private initiative. More recently, the Labour government under Blair and Brown has given us choice-based policies but also the Respect Agenda and Anti-Social Behaviour Orders aimed at making individuals more responsible.

All of these policies were introduced with a wave of publicity and positive rhetoric. The housing profession bought into them and dutifully sought to implement the changes the government required. Yet so few of these policies actually achieved anything real: many of my students have not even heard of Tenants' Choice. But then there is no need to worry because each of these initiatives is quickly superseded by the next big idea which is accompanied by a new wave of enthusiasm. Everyone buys into the new policy and any negative response is seen as cynical and divisive. We have no option, we are told, but to take up this exciting new idea. The housing profession and commentators soon get wrapped up in the detail and the new jargon created and, because it is new and different, we see it as significant and transformative.

Yet one policy did actually have the influence that was expected of it; indeed, it might be said to have superseded expectations. One policy achieved all that the government intended and radically transformed the structures of housing provision and the perceptions that we have of the various tenures. This policy not only achieved its desired effect, but has also been long-lasting. The policy was introduced in 1980, before any of those discussed above, yet it still has an impact, it is still in use and, moreover, it is likely to remain in place. This policy, of course, is the Right to Buy (RTB).

The RTB is the most successful housing policy in Britain since the Second World War. This is a very big claim and needs some substantiating. First, we can suggest it unequivocally met its avowed aims. The RTB was aimed at extending owner occupation to working-class households and breaking the hold of municipal socialism over public housing, and it succeeded in doing so. It has transformed housing in Britain and completely changed the manner in which the main housing tenures are perceived. Second, if popularity equates with success, then again the RTB scores highly. It helped the Conservatives to win a General Election with a reasonable majority in 1979 and by a landslide in 1983. The policy was, and remains, popular with tenants and the general public alike, so again we can suggest it is a success. Third, we might suggest that a policy that is so long-lasting must have had some success. After 30 years the RTB is still having an influence and, as far as these things are ever certain, it is impossible to repeal.

However, we also need to recognise the huge controversy that has surrounded the RTB ever since it was first mooted in the mid- to late 1970s. Even as it remains popular with many tenants and most politicians, we need to be aware why it has proved to be so unpopular in some quarters, particularly academics, housing commentators and, of course, certain elements of the housing profession. When the policy was announced and first implemented the Labour Party opposed it vociferously and made the RTB's repeal a focus of its 1983 election campaign. Many academics will point to the increase in homelessness in the 1980s and to the residualisation of council estates as directly caused by the RTB. The RTB, it is argued, reduced the ability of local authorities to help those in priority need, with the best properties being taken away by the most affluent tenants.

Of course, all of these comments can be countered with strong arguments: homelessness declined in the 1990s even though the RTB remained and stock numbers continued to fall; and RTB dwellings remained in exactly the same place with the same people living amidst the council tenants. Also by the 1987 General Election the Labour Party had become reconciled to the RTB and since then all the major parties have supported it and see it as a major part of their housing policies: all parties wish to claim they have increased owner occupation and particularly to working-class families (DOE, 1987; 1995; DETR, 2000; CLG, 2007). Yet, still for many the RTB is seen as an unalloyed disaster, and we will need to take seriously the criticisms that have been levelled against it.

But I want to concentrate not on the old criticisms of the RTB, but on what is a new challenge to it. This, of course, is the virtual collapse of housing markets in the UK since 2007. Indeed, the very source of the credit crunch is instructive to any discussion on extending owner occupation to working-class and low-income households. The start of the world financial crisis was the unravelling in 2006–07 of the sub-prime housing market in the US (Ferguson, 2008; Shiller, 2008). This very market was part of an attempt by American politicians to extend owner occupation as widely as possible. Ever since the Carter administration in the 1970s, lenders have been encouraged to lend to poorer households as part of a drive to extend the property-owning democracy that has been a staple of US populist rhetoric since the 1930s (Ferguson, 2008). But this lending has proved to be catastrophic for the households themselves, who have been unable to cope with increasing interest rates and falling house values, and for world financial markets that have traded on derivatives based on these sub-prime mortgages (Shiller, 2008; Wolf, 2009).

This is not the place to discuss the causes of the 2008 financial meltdown, but it does suggest that encouraging low-income households into owner occupation might be problematic; and what is the RTB about if not encouraging low-income households to become home owners? Indeed, the problems with housing in the UK since 2007 have led certain groups, such as the National Housing Federation, and politicians, mainly of the left, to question the continuation of the RTB (Beattie, 2008). What place, they argue, is there for a policy that allows households to purchase a dwelling owned by the state at a considerable discount whilst many of their fellow citizens are having their houses repossessed? The state should be providing more social housing, not allowing it to be reduced by the RTB. In this light the RTB can be seen to be privileging certain households – who might once have been in serious housing need, but now seem to have a reasonable income – at the expense of those suffering at the sharp end of the recession.

The government has been quick to defend the RTB as part of its long-term housing strategy, but this questioning in the face of an undoubted economic crisis does mean we have to be fully aware of what role the RTB has had, and continues to have, in the UK. Is it a policy whose time has gone? Over 2.5 million households have been assisted into owner occupation, but that was when the economy was functioning properly and houses could be bought and sold, rather than the stagnant markets of 2008–09. Can we still justify such a policy in the light of this crisis? Even if we might have supported it in the 1980s and 1990s, when many felt unable to access owner occupation in any other manner, can we afford to be so sanguine now when social housing waiting lists are growing and first-time buyers are excluded from the market?

Clearly this poses a challenge to those who see merit in the RTB, and it is one that needs to be faced head-on. In this book it is my intention to consider the RTB in the context of a financial crisis and a stagnant housing market. This will mean that my focus is not so much on the old controversies and criticisms of the RTB – those battles have been fought and won – but on what place there is for the RTB when housing markets appear to be failing badly and social housing is residualised and marginalised.

My main aim in this book is to explore why the RTB has been so successful despite the level of opposition to it. Just why was the RTB able to catch the imagination of both politicians and households? And why has it become so entrenched in British culture: is it because of the financial incentives, or because social housing was so bad, or is it because of something more positive and intrinsic in the relation between households and their dwelling? Does this mean that the RTB can ride out the current problems in the housing market and remain one of the means of encouraging working-class households into owner occupation?

We can, indeed, pose some more general questions, because the RTB was not an end in itself but a means to extend owner occupation. So, we might ask, why is owner occupation so appealing to households who for generations had rented their housing? In modern Britain, after nearly a century of public housing, why is it seen as so important to own your own home?

One way of opening up some of these issues is by looking at a couple of families who bought their council house in the 1980s. This will shed some light on what it meant to become an owner-occupier, and to see what changed and, equally important, what did not as a result of the RTB. These two families have been neighbours on a large council estate in Peterborough since the mid-1960s. The estate, which was built in the early 1960s, consists largely of three-bedroomed semi-detached houses built in streets and culs-de-sac. Both couples are now retired and their children have grown up and long since left. They have seen the area change around them as their neighbours, like them, bought their dwellings in the 1980s. Both families could be called 'respectable' working class in that they had worked all their lives, saved and made no recourse to state benefits.

T and J, in 40 years of living in the one dwelling, only changed things when they had to. For many years the house remained as it was when the council owned it: the same windows and doors; they kept the kitchen as it was when the house was new until the units finally needed replacing. They still had the walk-in pantry rather than knocking it through to the kitchen, as well as the indoor shed which could also have been used to extend either the kitchen or the lounge. The house was configured in a particular way when it was built: it worked for them and so why should they change it? The house was comfortable and they could look after it and make full use of it. T and J had enough money, at least in later life, to live how they pleased. This, however, did not include doing anything to the house unless it needed it.

Their neighbours, M and I, had altered their house – originally a mirror image of T and J's three-bedroomed council house – beyond recognition. They had put in new windows, made internal structural changes, built a conservatory, landscaped the front and back gardens, as well as seemingly always decorating inside and out. The house seemed to be their project, one that remains ongoing. In terms of the two households the main difference was in age – T and J in their 80s and M and I in their 60s – yet both had acted as they had done for many years. It was not that T and J had slowed down with age – they were using their dwelling in the same way now as they had 40 years ago when the council owned it. Both couples had raised children and seen them leave; both could be described as respectable working-class families. Yet they treated their dwelling quite differently.

The reason for the difference between the two is not financial, as when T and J wished to replace windows, carpets, change the kitchen units, and so on, they did so. They could afford to spend money on their dwelling when they had to. Yet they only did so when it was sensible and manageable, when it had to be done rather than merely because it could be. M and I, however, had always been improving and altering their dwelling. It was not that they did it once, but they were always doing it. They always had a project to work on, even perhaps looking for new things to do.

However, what M and I did not do was move to a new house. Their concern was solely with *this* house, where they had lived for 40 years and raised their children and had got so thoroughly used to. So their ambition was limited to an extent: it was about working just on the one house, whilst other households might have moved on after doing one house up to their satisfaction. What M and I did not seem to be interested in was making money from their house. Rather they wanted to improve it and work on it as they saw fit.

T and J saw their dwelling as just a place to live rather than a project to improve. Both households could use the dwelling in the same way – as a place in which to relax, to keep themselves fed, to sleep, and so on. But one household was content with this, whilst the other wanted to do more; one was content with things staying the same, the other wanted change and development, transformation even.

T and J would have perhaps done little different, even if they had had a 'better' starting position in terms of money to spend. They would have perhaps made some changes but not seen it as a continuing project. This is speculation, but in their later years, at least, they were not short of money, but still did not seek to transform their house. Perhaps they only had enough in later life because of years of saving, of forgoing spending until some future time. But this itself shows an attitude in line with their current frugality and indicates a similar mentality throughout their married life. They are able to moderate their needs, to refrain from excess, to say 'no' and to be content with enough.

This is not to suggest that what M and I have done is in any way excessive or grotesque. It is merely that they like to change their dwelling from time to time and they are able to manage this. This makes their house look bright and new, and if DIY is their hobby, then why not? There is no moral distinction to be made here between these two neighbours, both living comfortably within their means and how they like, in the way that best suits them, supporting each other like good neighbours do, but also keeping a respectful distance, not prying and keeping themselves to themselves.

So affordability is not at the root of this distinction, in that both households have chosen how they wish to live. Neither have unlimited choices, and as they grow older their remaining choices are perhaps diminishing. But this is not because of finance. Both still live pretty much as they have done all their adult lives. What differs is the attitude they have towards their dwelling.

These two examples are not meant to be typical of all RTB households. Rather what they show is that there is no typicality; that beyond being former tenants of the council, RTB households are different, they choose to live differently, to use their dwelling differently, and see their dwelling as a means to meet their specific aims and not as part of any general pattern determined by politicians, councillors, academics or the media. They are doing what they feel is best for themselves and their families, taking advantage of a situation that has arisen not by their choosing (I have no idea who they voted for in 1979 and subsequently). This is the same sort of decision that parents might take about their child's schooling: what comes first is what is best for the child and for the family as a whole. If opportunities present themselves then they are taken and without any guilt, just as middle-class households take advantage of their ability to buy a house near a good school.

But these examples also start to account for the success of the RTB. It let many working-class households use their dwelling as they saw fit for the first time. Instead of being constrained by their landlord, they could now paint their dwelling how they liked, change it, improve it or even leave it be, and it was their problem and not an issue for others to interfere in. The RTB allowed households to be independent and act in the responsible manner that they were always capable of if only they had been allowed to.

What this shows is that the RTB operates in a different manner from all other housing policies enacted in the last 30 years. Like all other housing policies the RTB was imposed from the centre and did not arise out of any spontaneous uprising from tenants. It was undoubtedly popular and caught the mood of the country at the time, but it was introduced, like any other policy, through legislation in Parliament and implemented on the direction of ministers and by civil servants. It was imposed upon local authorities, but then so has been every other housing policy we might mention. But despite this, the effect of the RTB has been thoroughly different from any other policy. This is because it directly alters the level of control that households have over where they live. Other policies have sought to increase the level of choice households have and the amount of responsibility they have to show, but none of them have had anything like the success of the RTB. This is because the RTB has been the only policy where the control over housing is actually transferred permanently and unconditionally to the household.

My argument, which I shall seek to develop more fully in subsequent chapters, is that the RTB was so successful because it played on the fact that housing is essentially a private relation. We experience our dwelling as individuals living in small groups of people who we are very close to and who we have a responsibility towards. We share our dwelling with people who we love and care for and who reciprocate those feelings. Our dwelling is where we share our most intimate and private relations (King, 2004a). It is through owning our dwelling that we gain greater control over these private relations. It allows us to protect those things that are close to us: our loved ones, our treasured possessions, our memories and our privacy. It might be argued that we need not own a dwelling to feel secure and safe and to have stable relations with those we love and care for. This may be so, but ownership means that we are responsible and no one else, and that we can make the decisions ourselves without having to defer to others who have no personal stake in our household.

All other housing policies are based on social or collective notions of housing. Accordingly, most policies tend to be concerned with aggregates and standards (King, 1996). Housing is dealt with as an aggregate, as a stock of dwellings rather than *a* dwelling. Policies do not seek to differentiate between particular households or dwellings, but rather to see them as types to which standards, outcomes and costs can be attributed. Even policies that are intended to extend choice in housing are based on national standards and prescriptions that determine the scope and nature of choice households can experience (Brown and King, 2005). Choice is imposed, but control is still retained in that the choices are constrained because the central government and landlords set both the rules for expressing choice and the resources available (Brown and King, 2005; King, 2006b). Choice is therefore limited to what the government and landlords feel is appropriate. So households might be able to express a choice over what dwelling they wish to live in, but the decision of whether they may live there is still in the hands of their landlord, and once they do live there they are still constrained by the landlord's policies and practices.

The RTB was the only housing policy that concerned itself with the manner in which individual households could use their dwelling. Once they exercised their right, households were then able to use their dwelling as they saw fit, being restrained only by their income, their ambition and the general law of the land. The landlord could no longer direct their use, and this was because the key resource – the dwelling itself – was now under the direct control of the household. The *genius* of the RTB – the basis of its success – was that it connected with the aspirations of individuals rather than projecting an abstract view of what individuals are deemed to want. It did not seek to tell households what they wanted and how they should live. Instead the policy was based on the notion that individuals favour those things close to them and that they wish to protect and nurture those things that they know and love. The virtue of the RTB, therefore, is that it is anti-collectivist. It is about meeting private interests and aspirations rather than any social aim. This is the manner in which we use our dwellings, almost without thinking and is an obvious way of looking at housing for the vast majority. We may live in houses that are similar to each other and do similar things in them, but we see them as distinctive, separate and unique. This is because we see the dwelling as *ours*.

But there was also a further reason for the RTB which had little to do with the virtues of owner occupation, and we need to be upfront about this. The RTB was an explicit attack on council housing and the whole legitimacy of local authorities as providers of welfare. For the Conservatives, local authorities and the housing they provided were not the solution to 'the housing problem', but the key cause of the problem in the first place. Partly this was because social renting was seen as a poor substitute for owner occupation, but more fundamentally social housing was seen as trapping people into dependency on the state and effectively disabling them (Conservative Party, 1976). Council housing was a key example of state provision and of dependency, of a culture of others taking decisions for people and so disabling them so they were dependent on bureaucracies. Local authorities, it was argued, did things for people that they could and should do for themselves.

The Conservatives wanted to break the inertia at the heart of social housing; the idea that it was the councils' responsibility to find people a house and to provide a subsidised rent. The Conservatives argued that households needed to do no more than put themselves on the council waiting list and then wait for their turn. What the Conservatives felt they needed to do was to deal with this passivity and encourage households to make decisions for themselves. We might see it as a means of encouraging households to show their competence and capability for decision making.

The RTB drastically reduced the influence of councils by taking away a third of their housing and putting the erstwhile tenant in control of it. In so doing the

Conservatives sought to reframe the relationship between landlord and tenant placing local authorities on the defensive. They were the ones forced to respond to the demands of tenants and the central government. The Conservatives saw themselves as representing ordinary households against the monolithic and faceless bureaucracies of local authorities. Of course, this was not merely achieved by the RTB, but involved other policies and spending cuts, although the RTB was the keystone in this attack on the role of local authorities.

But also council housing was the most manifest example of municipal socialism and this was a particular target of the Thatcher government. As Berlinski (2008) points out, a key element of Thatcherism was the destruction of socialism as an electorally significant force in British politics, and the large council estates and tower blocks in Britain's major cities were the most visible result of socialism in Britain. We might argue about how socialist any Labour government in the 20th century actually was, but council housing was a practical example of 'really existing socialism' and was perceived as such by the Conservatives who, under Thatcher, saw it as their role to defeat socialism once and for all. Council housing was therefore a target and accordingly its perceived failings could be readily placed alongside the apparent virtues of owner occupation and weighed in the political balance.

I mentioned earlier that the RTB was a means to an end, and that end was the promotion of owner occupation. In truth, owner occupation should itself be seen as a means rather than an end in itself, the real end being how we are able to use our dwellings (King, 2004a; 2008). However, being subsidiary – a means to a means – is not to deny the significance of the RTB. It was one of the key ways in which owner occupation could be advanced quickly and affordably. Accordingly, the years between 1980 and 1997 saw a rapid increase in owner occupation, with a significant amount of this increase being working-class households who had previously limited their aspirations to renting. This, we must admit, was a considerable achievement by the Conservatives.

What is particularly impressive is that this change is a permanent one. Even if the RTB was to be abolished forthwith, its effects could not be undone. Over 2.5 million households have become owner occupiers and their dwellings are now integrated into housing markets. This has changed the landscape of Britain in a physical sense but also, and more importantly, culturally. Owner occupation is now so ingrained as the 'natural' tenure that any other form of tenure is almost unthinkable to a majority of households. Most individuals in Britain do not consider social housing as an option even if eligible for it (most households not being seen as vulnerable or in priority need). The RTB is part of this transformation, which for most people is seen as both permanent and positive. To reverse the effects of the RTB would be the work of a generation if not longer and in any case could only be precipitated by some major cultural shift away from owner occupation, perhaps caused by some economic catastrophe. Now at the time of writing (March 2009) the possibility of a major catastrophe in housing markets cannot absolutely be ruled out, with the Brown government having completely or partially nationalised several banks, and house prices dropping by their largest percentage in 30 years. Yet we only have to look at the government's response to this crisis to see how unlikely it is that there will be any cultural shift away from owner occupation. A condition of the Brown government's bank bailout in 2008 was that the banks offered lending to households on the same terms as in 2007, that is, before the market started to decline. In addition, the government announced a scheme whereby up to 30% of the purchase price of a dwelling could be provided by an interest-free loan by the government. The funding for this scheme was to come from the existing funding for social housing. What is clear, therefore, is that the government will go a long way to support owner occupation. The scale of the meltdown of financial and housing markets would therefore have to be of an almost unimaginable scale before there is any fundamental rethink in housing policy, and it would be despite the best efforts of the government to shore up owner occupation.

There has been a lot written about the RTB since the later 1970s, some of which is positive and some that is negative. What is interesting is that most of the positive discussion does not come from housing experts but from those writing more generally about changes to British society and government. However, the view from the apparent experts, from within the housing studies bubble, is almost entirely negative. We might suggest that this is because experts are more knowledgeable about the issues and can see them more clearly. But it might mean that they are too close and too attached to a particular way of seeing housing issues that they cannot perceive things in any other manner. If we are concerned with social provision, as most housing academics and commentators are, then we will tend to see the RTB as a threat and as destructive. But I would also point to a further reason: academics, in the social sciences and humanities in particular, tend to see the current set of social arrangements as contingent, rather than accept them as how the world is. They are more likely to see social change and even transformation as possible, necessary and desirable.

However, commentators from outside the world of housing research can take a more rounded view and see the changes to housing policy in a wider context. We might suppose they are more likely to see owner occupation and a concern for housing markets as normal, as they recognise that this is what dominates housing discourse from electoral/political and cultural perspectives. In this sense they will not necessarily see current social arrangements as contingent, but rather 'just how things are'.

Moreover, the majority of households do not usually analyse housing markets and systems but merely seek to use their housing. They would then tend to see their housing in a self-interested manner, whereas those who earn a living from it will see it in more fundamental terms and be prepared to question, even if these questions are often ignored by the majority, and if no ready and practical answers are forthcoming.

The focus of this book is not on the structures of housing provision, or the particular interests of organisations, or indeed the notion of housing as a standardised aggregate (King, 1996). The RTB, we need to remember, imposed a duty on certain landlords to sell their dwellings to eligible tenants, but it did not insist that any tenant exercise their right. The policy gave individuals a choice: to commit to buying, or to stay as they were. It did not impose a particular position on any tenant, but merely facilitated, and encouraged, a particular action. The encouragement, we might argue, was not negligible, but two thirds of tenants were able to resist. Households only exercised their right to buy because they chose to, because they felt they could and should. They did not reject their dwelling or their immediate environment, but rather they literally bought into them. We need to understand this rather than just focusing on the general or aggregated effects of the policy. Likewise, we need to guard against the tendency to caricature or even demonise those households who bought their dwelling, or to see them as the dupes of a cynical and manipulative government. To hold these views is to reduce individuals to mere ciphers, to simple elements that can be controlled by the right form of stimuli. It is a patronising view that somewhat perversely demonstrates a rather unpleasant view of social tenants as people incapable of making decisions for themselves or of seeing what is in their best interests.

What I take very seriously in this book is the link between ideas and policies. It is my belief that the RTB can be linked very closely to a body of ideas and an understanding of human aspirations which is commonly called conservatism. What I consider important about the RTB is not well covered in the existing literature, or even given that much credence: this is an understanding of the RTB from a conservative perspective. What I seek to do in this book is to wrest the initiative back and to discuss the policy on what might be termed 'home' ground, rather than within an agenda set by others, who are almost uniformly hostile to the RTB. I want to link the RTB to ownership and conservatism but in a way that is free from the ideological baggage of the social democratic consensus that dominates serious discussion on housing.

Therefore I spend a considerable amount of time in this book exploring these ideas and making the links to the policy. I find it surprising that there is so little interest in conservative ideas when these have dominated actual policy making in the UK since 1979. One need not be a conservative to write about these ideas, but *not* being a conservative should not give one licence to ignore them. It is my belief that we cannot understand housing policy without also appreciating the ideas that lie behind it (King, 2006a). Consequently I see one of my main roles as exploring the ideas that lie behind the RTB and how these link with broader political, ideological and cultural themes.

My approach here might be seen as a fundamental approach, in the sense of seeking to understand what the policy aimed to do, what it derived from and why, and only then looking at its impact and its critics. In essence, this involves deliberately 'decontextualising' the policy so it can be understood on its own terms before then plugging it back into its broader policy context. This, inevitably, can only be partially achieved – the RTB to an extent was a reaction against other policies and practices – and such an approach obviously needs to be done rigorously and carefully so as not to slip into polemic and mere defensive justification. But this approach, done properly, does allow for a different and, I would argue, more satisfying and complete analysis of the RTB that does not automatically accept the baggage of the last 30 years of critique.

This point was for me the key: I wished to go beyond the critique that has built up, and to question the conventional view within housing studies and to connect up with a more fundamental debate on the role of individuals and the state. The RTB was a key element in the operationalisation of this dichotomy, and it can be seen as an experiment in relations between individuals and the state, as an attempt to extend individual capabilities and withdraw the influence of the state. It is this that makes the RTB so totemic, but which can so easily be lost in a debate that takes the efficacy of social housing for granted and which judges all policies in terms of the impact it has on the integrity of social housing.

This is not an attempt to divorce the RTB from Thatcherism, but rather the reverse. I want to separate the RTB from the rest of housing policy and to connect it to its ideological, political and cultural contexts. In this manner we can see the very *genius* of the policy: the idea of releasing an asset to individuals which they felt was already theirs, but which they were unable to control fully. The dwelling was the store of memory they call 'home' (King, 2004a), but which was not yet fully theirs to use and pass on, to complete those memories as they would wish. The RTB allowed them to 'absorb' the dwelling fully, to bring together the existential and the material, the human and the economic, the private and public.

As should now be clear, this book is also different from much of the existing literature in that it can be said to offer a rather more positive approach towards the RTB than is generally the case. This is not an uncritical discussion of the policy, but rather an attempt to be more rounded and to understand the RTB in a way that has been lacking in the housing literature. There are many who contest the legitimacy of the RTB and I wish to respond to this challenge and show the positives (as well as the negatives) and to explain just what appeal the RTB had, and continues to have. The RTB cannot simply be wished away or delegitimised through contempt. It has transformed housing policy in the UK and this, as I stated earlier, cannot be undone.

What I wish to do is to reach an understanding of just why the RTB was so successful in achieving its aims of widening owner occupation and reducing the scale and impact of social housing. One does not have to agree with a policy to seek to appreciate its effects. But this cannot be done by an overly critical and closed approach to the policy. We have to be open to what the RTB was for and what it achieved. So this book is an attempt to describe and assess the anatomy of the RTB as a piece of ideologically inspired and populist policy making. This means addressing the ideological underpinning in some detail to appreciate the ideas from which the policy derives and how it connects with a particular understanding of the human condition and our place in the world.

The second part of the subtitle of this book is therefore very important: we cannot appreciate the RTB without coming to terms with the desire to own that many of us have. This may be cultural rather than anything intrinsic, and it may be reinforced by policy and rhetoric, but the RTB did not come from nowhere. The RTB was not just the idle whim of some policy geek seeking to tinker with the fabric of public policy. Rather the policy was intended to connect with the desires of millions of households, who wanted to own, but felt they could not, and who felt they were being prevented from doing so. We can say that the RTB succeeded in this attempt. This book, therefore, is not a straightforward descriptive account of the policy, but rather an in-depth analysis of why the policy worked, and in presenting this analysis the book seeks to redress the balance of coverage on the policy.

I have no doubt that the approach taken in this book will be seen as controversial and many will find its arguments difficult to accept. This, I would suggest, is because it does not accept the consensus of housing studies, but rather adopts the 'consensus' – the normal, non-contingent, accepted view – that exists outside in the world beyond housing research and comment. I take the policy seriously rather than adopting the standard position of denigrating the RTB because of its purported impact on social housing. The book takes the RTB on its own terms, looking seriously at what the policy was intended to achieve and why it worked as it did. Instead of concentrating on what effects the policy had on other areas of housing, I want to look at the RTB *for itself*, with a sympathetic attitude that appreciates the RTB's cultural and political significance. This will be controversial, but I believe it is necessary to redress the balance and to show what the RTB really was about. Once we have done this we can then attempt to draw out the more general lessons of the RTB to inform public policy in the future.

The book is structured so that it begins with a narrow focus and slowly broadens out to consider the impact of the RTB and what we can learn from it. Chapter 2 provides the conceptual underpinning for the RTB, and considers the nature of conservatism and how this links to property ownership. This shall show how the RTB fits into an established set of ideas about the role of property ownership and how this links to personal responsibility and self-reliance, but within an ordered social whole. This discussion on responsibility is extended into a discussion of the concept of *really private finance*. This concept is used to capture the manner in which we seek to control and use our own resources to meet our own needs, aspirations and expectations. This capability is facilitated and enhanced by property ownership.

Chapter 3 looks at what actually happened with the RTB. It does this by assuming that the Conservatives were sincere in their intentions. It then discusses the specific ideas used by the Conservatives to justify the RTB. Finally, the chapter considers what the policy actually consisted of. So this chapter deals not just with what the Conservatives did, but what they actually meant by it. Chapter 4 then looks at the impact of the policy in terms of the numbers and types of properties sold. It goes on to consider whether the RTB caused the residualisation of social housing or whether a more complex situation existed where several policies came together to affect social housing. The chapter also looks at who the RTB was for and why it has declined in recent years.

Chapter 5 deals with the range of criticisms of the RTB and seeks to answer them. It considers what might be called the old criticisms of the RTB, those dating back to the 1980s, before moving on to look at perhaps the oldest of all, the notions of property ownership as false consciousness. However, we shall see how, in this post-Marxist age, this position has been modernised into a critique of ideology as hegemonic discourse. We will then move to consider some of the financial issues surrounding the RTB, although this will only be brief and there is no attempt to undertake a full financial analysis. The chapter then considers what might be termed 'friendly fire', those criticisms from the right that see the RTB as social engineering or that see any form of subsidy to owner occupation as a skewing of market mechanisms. Finally, the chapter looks at what might be seen as the new criticisms of the RTB brought on by the collapse of the housing market in 2008.

Chapter 6 considers what lessons we can learn from the RTB. In particular, was the RTB just a matter of lucky circumstance, or can we see it as an example of forward planning and clear thinking? Having done this I make some brief comments on what the history of the RTB tells us about social housing. Next the chapter considers why the policy worked and what we can learn from it in terms of general policy making and issues specific to housing. This leads to a consideration of what is the essence of the RTB: its direct link to the manner in which we use our housing. The chapter ends with a statement of some core principles fundamental to the RTB. The book ends with a brief conclusion that summarises some of the main points and tries to suggest what was so special about the RTB.

It might be said, therefore, that my aim is not to be balanced but to *redress the balance*. What I offer here is a full, considered and critical position, but one that does not start with the same preconceptions as the consensus view of the RTB. It assumes that the RTB is the most successful of housing policies, and thus provides a framework by which we can seek to understand the policy-making process and how it connects with the aspirations and desires of individuals. It is a study of how policy can seek to go with the grain of these desires rather than seeking to deny them. It is a study of what a former prime minister termed 'what worked'.

Note
Throughout this book I reserve the lower case for the general conservative ideology and the upper case for the political party.

TWO

Owning and using things

Introduction

The controversy over the Right to Buy (RTB) is essentially about ownership and where that ownership is vested. Partly this is because ownership in Britain is seen as important in itself, but also it relates to the manner in which owned things can be used and who determines that use.

It is also a concern for what ownership *means*. What is the significance of a stock of dwellings being held collectively and for a specific purpose which is itself deemed social, compared to a dwelling that is owned by an individual, that is to say, privately?

Another way of looking at this issue is to consider who the housing is for. Is the housing for the particular household who lives in it; that it exists for their benefit and to further their current and future ends? Or is housing a communal or social resource, which exists for some social purpose that might go beyond the interest of any individual household?

Yet another way of perceiving this issue is to ask the question: what can we do for ourselves and what do we expect from others, in particular, the state? Are we responsible for ourselves and our loved ones, and so have to ensure that we can look after them, or is this limited by what society feels is a good life? Can we be limited by what the state thinks is good for us?

We can, of course, see this argument in several ways: the past versus the present; the present versus the future; individuals versus society. Some or all of these interests might coalesce. But equally we can see them as antagonistic and conflictual.

Yet however we frame the debate, we can see that it is quite fundamental to the nature of housing and the manner in which it is controlled. Ownership, either as a stock of dwellings, or as individual dwelling units, as social or private, is central to the manner in which we seek to debate and understand housing.

These statements represent a particular view of housing. It is what we might see as British, or more specifically Anglo-Saxon. It is the view that takes property to be central to the nature of housing markets and housing policy. It need not, of course, be the only way in which we view housing – many European countries are seemingly less concerned with the ownership of their housing stock – but it is the manner, I would argue, in which housing in the UK and the Anglosphere countries is viewed and must be understood. This position, I want to suggest, is essentially a conservative one, which depends upon a particular set of cultural conditions that derives from individualism and a trust in certain tried and tested institutions and the rule of law. This position will undoubtedly appear uncongenial to some and even anachronistic after more than a decade of Labour government, but I see it as pivotal to any understanding of the success of the RTB. Indeed, the opposition to this conservative position, as expressed in arguments against owner occupation and the RTB in particular, can be said merely to demonstrate the centrality of ownership to our understanding of contemporary housing policy in the UK.

This chapter seeks to justify this argument and, in doing so, to provide the theoretical underpinning for the understanding of the RTB. Of course, on one level, the appeal of the RTB was very basic and, indeed, we might argue that it panders to rather 'base' instincts such as greed and self-interest. This, though, is a difficult argument to sustain. It assumes that individuals can be manipulated by basic stimulus–response mechanisms and that humans are motivated solely by economics and personal financial advantage. If this were true it would deny the possibility of solidarity and altruism, and so question the very possibility for any truly *social* housing.

But despite this we could certainly maintain that the RTB has little to do with ideas and more to do with money. However, as I will show in this chapter, the concept of property ownership is the one area in which conservatism really does engage with abstract ideas. This, I want to suggest, is because conservatives see some strong conceptual link between the practicalities of property ownership and the form of social order they are in politics to maintain. The RTB can be seen as an important, and practical, means of attaining that political goal, and as such it is not only legitimate, but essential, for us to come to terms with the manner in which the political pursuit of greater personal ownership of things relates to a consistent and coherent body of ideas.

One of the problems with the way in which the RTB has been discussed is that it tends to focus on the effects of the policy. What tends to be lacking is any sense of what ownership means for individuals. I want to show that, whilst financial incentives were clearly an element in the success of the RTB, it is too simplistic to suggest that the policy depended just on money. Owner occupation has a tremendous appeal and this has been a consistent theme of post-war British politics. It is tempting to suggest that there is something intrinsic to this appeal, and that it might relate to human nature. However, as Saunders (1990) has shown, this is a complex and difficult area which tends towards a controversy that we cannot hope to resolve here. I therefore am not seeking to argue that owner occupation is 'natural', in the sense of relating to something innate to human beings: there is no genetic predisposition to ownership.

However, something need not have a genetic basis for it to appear natural. It may be that certain social arrangements are so ingrained, are such a part of the social structure, that any alternative form of social organisation is untenable. As Hayek (1978; 1988) has argued, institutions that have developed over many generations and as a result of gradual evolution rather than design, can be seen as 'natural' in the sense of deriving unintentionally out of human action. These institutions are not natural as we would understand them in the physical sciences but are rather *epistemologically objective.* This term has been coined by Searle (1995), who argues that certain institutions or arrangements can be all too objective, in that we cannot avoid them or simply wish them away, whilst still being the result of human practices. These institutions have arisen as a result of the particular organisation of human society, which could, in other circumstances, be differently organised. They are therefore, according to Searle (1995), *ontologically subjective*, in that their being need not have taken that specific form, or indeed need not have come into being at all. However, once these institutions do exist in the way they do we cannot avoid them and so they are an objective part of our understanding of the world. Hacking (1999) provides a useful example of Searle's distinction when he sees rent payment as epistemologically objective, in that if we wish to stay in the dwelling we must pay rent. However, rent is also ontologically subjective 'because without human subjects and their institutions there would be no such object as rent' (p 22). We can readily imagine a world without rent, and without private property, but once it is there and so intrinsically established in our world, it can appear to be natural, as the way the world just is.

I want to assert that owner occupation arises out of a particular cultural condition which determines the nature of politics in the UK. This cultural condition is small-'c' conservatism, which places at its centre the desires to keep things close and to maintain control over our immediate environment. We might suggest that this cultural condition arises from a particular *understanding* of human nature that we can call conservative. The way in which this cultural condition is manifested is through what I have chosen to call *really private finance*. This is the idea that we determine the use of our resources on the basis of our own needs, aspirations and expectations. I want to suggest that we have a predisposition to keep certain people and things close to us and through this desire we make sense of the world. It is this predisposition, mixed with historical accidents, geography and other factors, that has created the particular set of institutions on which our current notions of property ownership are based.

A particular obstacle to a sensible debate on the RTB is the refusal of its opponents to see that it might be underpinned by anything serious. Partly this is because these critics refuse to see anything serious and intellectually demanding in the very notion of conservatism. There is this assumption that intellectuals are by definition socialist or left-wing and that there has been no serious thought from the right. Of course, this position is self-fulfilling: if right-wing thought is not serious we need not read it, and so there is no serious right-wing thought.

But refusing to look at something does not make it go away, and whilst the left has been parading its intellectual credentials the right have actually been running things. Left-wing ideas have not been acceptable to the British electorate since the mid-1970s. Those on the left with more interest in doing things than just thinking and plotting have cottoned on to this and realised that to seek power they need to learn and borrow from the right. In doing so they might be equally as popular, and this indeed proved to be the case with the election of the Blair government in 1997. The result of this has been to isolate the academic left from any political influence. Their disdain and purity has meant that it is the right that now dictates the terms of political debate, be it on issues like the role of the market, trade union rights or, of course, housing tenure.

This consistent domination of practical politics, whereby the Labour Party is only electable if it can present a conservative face, could not be sustained were it not for something serious and coherent behind it. Conservative ideas could not have been so dominant without there being some solidity to them which appeals to a broad spectrum of the public. These may not be found in wordy treatises or stated as overt social theories, but they are part of a serious intellectual position nonetheless.

What conservative thinkers pride themselves on is the manner in which their ideas connect with the practicalities of ordinary life. Conservative ideas, according to Scruton (2000), contend with the extrinsic aspects of life. These ideas deal with the surface of things rather than what is deemed to be underlying. This extrinsic sense connects to key ideas such as the importance of self-interest in our decision-making behaviour; personal responsibility for ourselves and for those we love and care for; and the expectations we have for ourselves and our children. This extrinsic sense is therefore about how we can relate to the persons and things around us and so understand the world in which we inhabit through no choice of our own.

These ideas are extrinsic precisely because they seek to connect us with a sense of what is practical and possible. There is no concern here with abstractions and a sense of what could be if only we were of a different nature or kind. Rather, these notions of self-interest, responsibility and expectation are grounded in our lived experiences. They denote a concern for things on the surface; of an immediacy of experience and response. It is the very opposite of the utopianism and speculation at the heart of much leftist ideology. The conservative view accepts what is epistemologically objective as the only sense of objectivity that there can be.

Conservative thought is a concern for things that are close to us: those we love and who share our lives; those objects and possessions that allow us to protect those we love and maintain our closeness; and for those relations that tie us in and protect us and others so we can be free to pursue our own ends safely. These are important ideas, and they are capable of being expressed with a high degree of abstraction as we can see in the writings of such significant conservative thinkers as Gottfried (1986) and Voegelin (2002). Yet they are ideas that are grounded and which connect with individuals at an almost instinctual level. As Scruton suggests, these ideas run with human beings as they are (or appear to be) rather than how they ought to be. They do not promise a brighter future through sacrifices today; they do not ask us to forgo everything for the possibility of a better tomorrow. Rather these ideas are about how we can and do live now.

It is my experience that most housing academics, for the reasons stated earlier, are rather ignorant of conservative thought. Indeed, they may well actually take this ignorance as a badge of honour. Yet also most of these academics are owner-occupiers, who think about the needs of their families, quite rightly putting them first in their plans and decision making. They quite properly take responsibility for their actions and take decisions which are aimed at ensuring that they and their loved ones prosper. This is precisely what conservative thinkers suggest that they would do, and it is why conservative thought is so much more significant than the left would have us believe. Conservative thought actually derives out of an understanding of what real people do in real-world situations.

This last statement will be treated by most with scepticism or derision, and so it needs some justification. Therefore in this chapter I wish to explore the nature of ownership and to link this with conservatism as the dominant ideology in British – or English[1] – political life. The chapter moves from the general to the (more) specific and from the abstract to the (more) practical. It begins with a discussion on the nature of conservatism, aiming to provide a brief definition of the ideology and how it differs from other political ideas in certain respects. Second, it considers the nature of ownership as one of the most significant elements in conservative thought. This, of course, is especially relevant to our study of the RTB and its impact. I want to show how the RTB fits into an established set of ideas about the role of property ownership and how this links to personal responsibility and self-reliance, but within an ordered social whole. This discussion on responsibility is extended in the third section of this chapter, where the concept of *really private finance* is introduced and discussed. This concept is used to capture the manner in which we seek to control and use our own resources to meet our own needs, aspirations and expectations. This capability is facilitated and enhanced by property ownership.

This chapter seeks to provide the conceptual underpinning to the study of the RTB. My view is predicated on the sense that the RTB is not just a piece of political opportunism but a policy that has a considerable resonance with many households, linking as it does with a particular understanding of human nature and the world. This perspective is undoubtedly a conservative one, but it is, I wish to contend, also the default position for most of us. So what I am trying to do is present the RTB from the perspectives of individuals, and not just as a piece of public policy that affects landlords and 'housing' in general. This will help us to see why the policy had, and retains, an almost visceral appeal and tends to be opposed only by those with some interest in the institutional integrity of social housing.

The conservative position

Conservatism, it is often said, is somewhat different from other political ideologies (Quinton, 1993; Scruton, 2001). Indeed, some might see it as not really an ideology at all. Now this is, of course, a dangerous tack to take. Both Marxists and classical liberals have suggested that their positions are criticisms of ideology, and that *they* are immune to the vice of ideology themselves. We can suggest that this is both a convenient position and an unconvincing one. Both Marxism and classical liberalism are normative social theories seeking to justify a particular form of social organisation. They are, to use the definition of Adams (1993), a set of beliefs that one accepts and uses to justify one's actions. These beliefs rest on some normative principles which cannot be gainsaid or further underpinned. What they are not is a science or rational critique that stands above or beyond the cut and thrust of belief and opinion.

With this in mind, I do not want to suggest that conservatism is not an ideology. There is a set of beliefs which can generally be referred to as conservatism, even if these are rather broad. But these beliefs are somewhat different in type from those held by other ideologies. Therefore, it is not merely that conservatives believe in different things than Marxists or liberals, it is rather a matter of ambition and scope. Unlike other ideologies, including libertarianism or classical liberalism that it is sometimes associated with, conservatism is not necessarily concerned with ends, but rather with processes. It is an ideology concerned with means. It does not have a particular end, other than that of good government. Accordingly, conservatism is wary of the notion of abstract theorising, of the universal statement of where a particular society ought to be if it is to be called 'good'. As Quinton (1993) states, 'As an ideology conservatism is, then, procedural or methodological rather than substantive. It prescribes no principles or ideals or institutions universally and so falls outside the scope of its own rejection of abstract theory' (p 247). Conservative ideology therefore presents no model for how society should look, rather it is concerned with the means by which change both occurs and can be managed. Conservatism, indeed, involves a critique of abstraction and concerns itself instead with the means by which a society might thrive. In this way it is distinctly different from all other political ideologies which will usually assert a series of ends based on a number of specific principles.

The key distinction of conservative ideology is therefore that it is dispositional rather than patterning. It is a concern for processes rather than specifying outcomes. This being so, we can suggest that the conservative disposition might operate at three levels. First, individuals can be disposed towards conservatism, seeking to maintain their current position and defend what they hold dear. Thus apparently radical trade unionists might be better characterised as demonstrating a conservative disposition. This conservatism might not be a particularly political outlook: for instance we can see this disposition in certain parts of the Anglican Church, particularly in opposition to issues such as the ordination of women and homosexual men as priests.

Second, we can see conservatism as referring to actual policies and practices that are conservative. These we will often refer to as Conservative or Tory, giving a proper name to these policies and practices to place them in a particular historical and cultural context. Hence we can, and will, discuss the policies of the UK Conservative Party as a distinctive entity. There is a difficulty here, of course, in that some policies adopted by the Labour Party might be considered conservative, for example, supports to owner occupation, the Private Finance Initiative and so on (King, 2006a). Indeed, some policies which are pursued by the Conservatives in the UK might also be pursued by the Democratic Party in the US, for example, welfare reform. It might even be that some of the policies pursued by the Conservative Party are not particularly conservative, for example, the enforced abolition of grammar schools by the Heath government in the 1970s. What is important here, though, is that it is possible to see conservatism as being a tribal connection, or almost a defining label, so that one is a conservative because of one's membership of the Tory Party.

Third, we might see this conservative disposition as existing in general throughout a culture, where there is a general disposition towards tradition and recourse to established institutions and past precedent to influence the present. This, as Quinton (1993) argues, might coincide roughly with Weber's notion of political legitimacy being based on tradition rather than bureaucracy or charisma. What this suggests is that certain countries have political and cultural traditions that might be described as conservative, and all political parties seeking influence within that country must operate according to those restrictions, and this would apply regardless of the government in power and whether it considered itself in the least bit conservative. Clearly, this takes us beyond political ideology as such, and into the realms of political psychology and whether there is any such thing as national character (which, of course, is itself a conservative idea). However, my speculation is that British political culture in its generality[2] is conservative and therefore all political parties need – and want – to operate within this particular atmosphere.

Many will find the notion that there is a conservative political culture in the UK objectionable, and would doubtless point to the elections in 1997, 2001 and 2005 for support. But we need to appreciate that the differences between political parties in the UK are relatively minor. The disputes between them are on specifics, which of themselves may cause considerable controversy and argument, yet all parties accept the established procedures of politics. The means by which politics is done in Britain is established as a gradualist, piecemeal approach to change, all based on an understanding of the pluralism of ends. This is essentially a conservative approach, even if many of these changes are controversial and contested (not least by the Conservative Party itself).

Therefore, as I have argued elsewhere (King, 2006a), there has been a considerable continuity in UK housing policy since the 1970s, with a shift towards personal subsidies, the use of private finance and market disciplines and the promotion of owner occupation. Changes of government, therefore, have not been the decisive breaks that they are often portrayed to be by political parties. Instead there has been a conservative consensus in housing policy which has been shared by both the Conservative and Labour parties. Indeed, the longevity and security of the RTB is testament to this consensus.

The problem that many commentators will have in accepting this position is that the majority of them see the current political settlement as contingent. That is to say, they see the political structures in the UK as illegitimate and ripe for transformation, typically into some form of socialist state in which capitalist institutions are abolished or at least seriously contained. Many commentators on housing and social policy see the political spectrum as being much wider than is actually the case in practice, if we were to see electability and public support as the main criteria. The academy still has many radicals and revolutionaries amongst its number, and whilst they are safer there than in the real world, this does colour their approach to policy issues. What they are testing policies against are not the practicalities that concern elected politicians, but an abstract ideological position in which purity is seen as more important than applicability. But conservatism, to reiterate, is not an abstract ideological position; rather it is an engaged one. Moreover, it is engaged in the means of politics rather than the ends.

Yet immediately we are faced with a difficulty. When we consider recent Conservative governments, particularly those led by Mrs Thatcher which were responsible for the RTB, the terms that most readily spring to mind are those such as 'radical', 'divisive', 'committed' and 'controversial' (Berlinski, 2008). Indeed, Mrs Thatcher apparently at times viewed herself as a conservative revolutionary (Green, 2006). Her governments were noted for their activism, their strong sense of purpose and direction. One might disagree with that direction and see them as seriously misguided, but they were certainly purposive. From this we might want to suggest that conservatism is about strong actions and committed and purposeful leadership. Yet in many ways conservatism appears to stand for the opposite. It is not about ends, but is rather concerned with means. It does not stand for any clearly articulated set of principles.

In trying to deal with this apparent paradox, Giddens (1994) talks of a shift in political purpose between left and right. Those on the right, such as Thatcher and Reagan (and we can add the second President Bush to this list), became the radicals, eager to force through change, often against the will of established interests and institutions. Against this he suggests that parties and agencies who were erstwhile noted for their radicalism, such as the British trade union movement, environmentalists and Eastern European communists in the late 1980s, were now acting like reactionaries who sought to prevent or halt change. This leads Giddens to posit the concept of *philosophical conservatism*. This he sees as a general presumption against change, and a belief that current institutions need preserving. It is just that the institutions apparently in danger are those of the traditional left such as trade union rights, state control and environmental protection. It was the post-war settlement that appeared to be under threat by the Thatcher governments and thus 'radical politics' – as traditionally defined – became more about reacting to threats and protecting institutions than transforming society.

But as O'Hara (2005) has suggested, this was not really conservatism but simply a reaction to threats. We cannot assume that conservatism is simply a reaction to any change. What Thatcherites might well have argued is that radical and controversial changes were necessary in order to *preserve* something important: that the only manner in which society could be returned to its proper – conservative – nature was through changes that would appear divisive to many. This argument is familiar to conservatives since Burke (1999), who have seen change as necessary, but only as a means of preserving and maintaining those institutions we as a society see as crucial to our survival.

We might agree with O'Hara's critique, but what I find interesting about the idea of philosophical conservatism is that Giddens sees it not as a defined set of doctrines or dogma – it is not a political programme – but as an *attitude*, or a way in which individuals and groups are predisposed to respond to threats to their perceived interests. Even though we might want to dispense with Giddens' conclusions that trade unionists and environmentalists are in some way demonstrating conservatism, we need to admit that this notion of an attitude is precisely how conservative thinkers themselves would characterise their beliefs. Giddens, in this sense, has picked up on something elemental to conservatism.

Most writers on conservatism do not see it as a theory of society but as a *disposition*. It is a way of thinking and acting or having an attitude, which predisposes us towards certain responses. Hence Kirk (1985) can talk of *The Conservative Mind*, rather than a set of theories or a description of a utopia.[3] Fundamentally, conservatives like Kirk believe they are merely recognising and responding to how human beings are. And if Giddens is not prepared to go this far, he at least appears to recognise it as a disposition that, in some circumstances and on some occasions, even supposed radicals can be prey to.

But we still have not done any more than hint at what conservatism consists of: we need to be more specific. The problem in doing this, though, lies precisely in the fact that conservatism is not a set of doctrines. Indeed, as Scruton (2001) argues, it is seldom explicitly articulated by its adherents. He suggests that at one level we should not expect advocates of moderation to feel the need to articulate their views. Advocates of 'keeping things as there are' would quite naturally find themselves at a loss to explain why things should be this way. The adherents of conservatism, seen as having a general complacency with how things are and a concomitant reluctance to contemplate a movement away from the status quo, would find their position a self-evident one. Scruton states that conservatism 'is characteristically inarticulate, unwilling (and indeed usually unable) to translate itself into formulae or maxims, loath to state its purpose or declare its view' (2001, p 9).

But this does not mean that we should not try to define conservatism, nor that others have not tried to do so. The simplest definition would be to suggest that conservatives seek to *conserve*: they aim to keep things as they are. But, quite rightly, Scruton feels that just to state that conservatives have a desire to conserve is a rather limp definition. Unlike Giddens' notion of philosophical conservatism, what needs to be considered is what is to be conserved and why (O'Hara, 2005). It is not enough simply to say that we wish to conserve. We must qualify this by stating what we wish to maintain and why it is so important for us to do so.

What we are aiming to conserve are those things close to us and which we hold dear. So, for Scruton, 'conservatism arises indirectly from the sense that one belongs to some continuing and pre-existing social order, and that this fact is all-important in determining what to do' (2001, p 10). We feel ourselves to be part of some larger whole, which defines us as individuals. This social entity becomes mingled with the private lives of its members: 'They may feel in themselves the persistence of the will that surrounds them. The conservative instinct is founded in that feeling: it is the enactment of historical vitality, the individual's sense of the society's will to live' (Scruton, 2001, p 10). Expressed in this manner we can see why it might be unarticulated. Scruton sees it almost as a gut reaction, as something elemental.[4] Conservatism is about the relationship we have with those things around us, and in particular here with those social entities that form us and which we therefore identify with as defining our sense of self. As we shall see when we discuss Scruton's ideas on property and owning things, there is more than a hint of Hegelian idealism in this most English of conservatives. Scruton's connection between individual and social life appears to owe much to Hegel's conception of freedom as consecrated in the bond between individual and society, where we are only free to act because we are located within a social whole (Hegel, 1991).

Already at this stage, we can see that conservatism has a particular view of the individual. Individuals are defined in relation to something else, rather than the liberal view which sees individuals as being complete in themselves and where their qualities come, as it were, from within. Conservatives do not subscribe to the Kantian ideal of individuals being ends rather than means. This is not because they are against freedom of the individual, but rather they believe that one cannot be free unless one is surrounded by some set of social relations that allow one to operate. The important thing, though, is that conservatives look to things outside of themselves to define them as individuals: they are not sufficient unto themselves, but rely on social institutions and collective notions to sustain them.

Scruton sees the conservative instinct deriving from a need to feel connected to some pre-existing social order, and from a need to protect this sense of belonging. We can explore this further by trying to understand what conservatives might mean by this sense of pre-existence and continuity. Quinton (1993) suggests that there are three central elements in conservative thought: *traditionalism*, *scepticism* and *organicism*. These are all connected to this sense of continuity, but also inform us as to when and why change is necessary and acceptable, and how it should be attempted.

Traditionalism

This first element relates most directly to the rather simplistic view of conservatism as being about 'conserving' and a reaction to change. Quinton suggests that traditionalism is based on a support for continuity in politics, for the maintenance of existing institutions and practices and a suspicion of change. Where change is seen as necessary, it should be gradual and only undertaken after careful consideration: it should be evolutionary and piecemeal rather than fundamental and transforming. The ideal for a conservative would be a situation where change comes only in response to extra-political circumstances, such as population changes. The political arrangements of a community are, for the conservative, settled and permanent.

But the support for traditionalism does not derive merely from reactionary instincts or inertia (although there may be some of this), but from the instrumental effects of these long-standing practices and institutions. It is presumed that these would not have existed for so long without providing some considerable benefit to our ancestors and ourselves. Accordingly, Kekes (1998) identifies a conservative traditionalism that protects those institutions that allow individual autonomy to flourish. This tradition implies the limiting of governments' authority to interfere with these institutions. He sees a predisposition to institutional arrangements that promote individual autonomy and that the conservation of tradition serves to embed this sense of liberty. One such institution, of course, is private property rights, but we might also point to the rule of law and the mechanisms that ensure its enforcement.

Perhaps the most famous and elegant discussion of the virtue of traditions is that of Burke (1999), who stated that society is a partnership between the living, the dead and those yet to be born. A society is based on inherited patterns and traditions and the living have a duty to respect the interests of the dead and the unborn. This is because these patterns and traditions embody the interests of the dead and offer a prospectus to the unborn. One respects the dead by preserving and passing on what they have created to those yet to come. Thus social institutions are not *ours*, but are held in trust for future generations. This statement of Burke's is also important in its realisation of the organic nature of a society, a doctrine we shall consider below.

It is the sheer unpredictability of change that causes concern for conservatives. If we are unable to predict outcomes with any certainty, how can we rationally propose change? The issue is merely compounded by the fact that the current situation is known – we are aware of what existing institutions offer us, with all their imperfections – whereas the future is always hypothetical. Those with a utopian cast of mind would, of course, see the opposite possibility here, where the future is untainted by the ugly and imperfect present, but for a conservative this is mere wishful thinking. The conservative disposition is very much tied to the present, and if it is looking anywhere it is backwards. So where change is seen as necessary, it should be planned and gradual to ensure that any unplanned effects can be understood and, where necessary (and possible), countermanded. According to Scruton, in order to minimise the dangers involved, change should be continuous and gradual. So conservatism does not mean a rejection of change: 'The desire to conserve is compatible with all manner of change, provided only that change is also continuity' (Scruton, 2001, p 11). Change should only be actively embraced when it offers support to those institutions that are proven as beneficial.

This belief is based on experience, in that conservatives can point to many historical examples of bad changes, which have led to political upheaval, mass murder and even genocide. Since Burke's time in the late 18th century, conservatives have warned against the effect of utopian adventure in politics. From the conservative point of view, there have been far too many examples of bad changes to make anything acceptable other than changes which are piecemeal, controlled and evolutionary. This element of traditionalism links into the second key doctrine associated with conservatism.

Scepticism

The second key element of conservatism identified by Quinton (1993) is scepticism about political knowledge. This arises out of a traditional world view and also colours the conservative attitude to social change. Quinton argues:

> Political wisdom ... is embodied ... in the inherited fabric of established laws and institutions. This is seen as the deposit of a great historical accumulation of small adjustments to the political order made by experienced practitioners, acting under the pressure of a clearly recognised need in a cautious, prudent way. (1993, p 245)

Political wisdom is the accrual of very many tiny adjustments in the political realm. Politicians are seen as operating under the pressure of events, using their accumulated judgements to minimise the adverse consequences of these pressures, and to protect the essential elements within the political fabric. Politics is seen as being responsive and defensive rather than programmatic.

A sceptical attitude is seen as necessary because there are clear limits to what we can know about the political realm. Kekes (1998) suggests that conservatives are sceptical because, whilst we might seek to base political arrangements on a rational basis, there are distinct limits to reason. Conservatives, according to Kekes, do not reject rationality in political discourse. However, they do see it as limited and by no means a sufficient condition. There are limits to what can be planned rationally due to the inevitability of unintended consequences. Furthermore, conservatives point to the often bitter consequences of attempts at rational planning, or what might be seen less positively as social engineering. Conservatives are critical of mass social house building and town planning for the same reason (Boyson, 1978; Scruton, 2000).

This critique of rationality and its limitations is most closely associated with Oakeshott and his seminal essay *Rationalism in Politics* (1991). Oakeshott can be seen as an evolutionary conservative. He sees change as inevitable, but where it is necessary it should still be cautious. This is because the consequences of political action are unpredictable: rational planning is prone to failure, if not disaster.

Like Kekes, Oakeshott suggests that the purpose of social and civic institutions is to protect our traditional liberties, and these institutions might have to evolve so that these liberties can be preserved. If we are faced with new threats, be they due to globalisation, environmental pollution, demographic change or whatever, those institutions that protect the integrity of a society need to evolve to meet these new threats. Oakeshott is explicit on this evolutionary character, stressing that we develop social institutions out of practice rather than by design and planning. He is fundamentally opposed to rational planning as it demonstrates a misunderstanding of the operation of human experience. These ideas have a resonance here not only with the libertarian social philosophy of Hayek (1960; 1988) and Mises (1981), but also of both Heidegger (1962) and Wittgenstein (1958). Like these other thinkers, Oakeshott's critique is epistemological, in that it calls into question what we can know and, more importantly, what we need to know for us to be members of a viable polity. One gains knowledge of the world, and progresses through it, by action and not through rationalisation. This scepticism about human knowledge leads Oakeshott to see politics as a practice that is best performed by those experienced in governing.

There is a further strand to Oakeshott's thinking that is important here, and this is his belief in the need to clear the relationship between state and citizen. Like some libertarian thinkers, and particularly Hayek, Oakeshott argued that the role of intermediate institutions such as trade unions, the professions and local government needs to be tightly constrained to ensure that the proper relationship between state and citizen can be fostered and maintained (Devigne, 1994). This point is developed by Scruton (2001) who sees the relationship between state and citizen (or subject, as he would have it according to the British constitutional tradition) as similar to that of parent and child with the consequent reciprocity of fealty, submission and protection that goes with that relationship. It follows from this that institutions that insinuate themselves between the state and citizen are potentially disruptive to this relationship, bringing with them special and particular interests and grievances that might subvert the direct relation between citizens and their protector.

Scruton suggests, along with Oakeshott, that conservatives do not see any purpose in politics other than governing. We indulge in many activities as ends in themselves, and without any larger purpose. We go fishing, read books, watch films and have relationships with others. These activities are not derivative of anything, nor are they subservient. They are sufficient in themselves as ends. Likewise, as Scruton suggests, a society is already an end: 'Its history, institutions and culture are the repositories of human values' (2001, p 13). Society is not the means to achieve some future goal, but a worthy end in itself as it now exists. Individuals have interests, needs and ends *now*, and there is no reason why these should be sublimated to some future ends that may or may not be realised. Hence Scruton suggests that communism is absurd, as it is the condition where government is at war with the very people it has set out to govern: individuals are prevented from doing what they may wish to do now, in order to prepare 'the people' for some future utopian state in which the ends of others are imposed.[5]

Conservatives have an anti-contractual view of society, in that they believe in non-voluntary duties, allegiances and obligations. Society is not instituted through any social contract, rather human life is definitionally social and therefore there could never have been any state of nature or human existence outside of society.

Moreover, the ties that bind one to society are neither optional nor conditional. One has duties that override any individual predisposition.

What goes along with this scepticism about universalism is a pessimism that guards against false hopes and rejects the idea of human perfectibility (Kekes, 1998). Conservatives, being anti-utopians, do not believe that a perfect society is achievable or that evil and misfortune can be eradicated. Conservatives do not believe in progress, or that all situations are improvable. Muller (1997) identifies a belief in human imperfection and what he terms an *epistemological modesty*, in that there are limits to human knowledge. He suggests that conservatives place a dependence on institutions 'with their own rules, norms, restraints and sanctions' (1997, p 11). These institutions, however, are by no means transferable. Human beings rely on customary rules based on historical experience rather than the continual reinvention of social rules. Like Burke (1999), Muller uses the term 'prejudice' without it having any necessary pejorative connotation, but as a *prejudging* of a situation according to our habits, customs and experience. This leads on to further qualities identified by Muller, namely, those of historicism and particularism.

Perhaps the most common criticism of this sceptical approach is particularly relevant to our study of the RTB and so worth touching on here. This criticism is that support for the status quo is merely a disguise for protecting certain vested interests. Conservatism, it is said, is merely an attempt to preserve traditional institutions and liberties, and seeks to maintain the status quo as a position where one group is dominant. Honderich (1990), for example, argues that the aim of conservative ideology is merely to protect property ownership and existing property relations. Private property rights merely institutionalise existing inequalities. There is thus no particular merit in these institutions if all they do is to entrench property rights that exclude a large number of people. The response to this position is twofold. First, one way of characterising pluralism is as a *series* of vested interests which compete and which may not be reconcilable. The conservative position can be seen to an extent as agonistic, in that the multiplicity of interests within a society cannot always be reconciled. But conservatives such as Kekes (1998) would argue that there are some institutions that are better able to accommodate pluralism than others. Such conservatives would argue that the rule of law, private property and the protection of individual freedoms will best guarantee that no single interest supplants another. Having said this, in UK politics only one party actually identifies itself explicitly with an interest group, and that, of course, is the Labour Party.

The second response to the vested interest argument is that it is implausible to suggest that some institutions would have survived, and been maintained in the last century by all parties (including that of organised labour), without their having some utility for all groups. Indeed, it is a matter of fact that all parts of British society have prospered in absolute terms over the last century. What we appear to have, therefore, is a set of institutions in which the party of organised labour can pursue its vested interests without this having overly detrimental effects on other interests.

Organicism

The third doctrine identified by Quinton (1993) is the belief that human beings and society are organically or internally connected. Human beings are not fully independent of the social institutions and practices within which they grow up. We have seen this already when discussing Scruton's Hegelian sense of the conservative instinct. An individual's sense of self depends, in part at least, on his or her appreciation that they are part of a social whole. Moreover, this social whole is specific. They are not part of 'humanity' as such, nor is it the case that humans need to be part of *any* community. For the conservative what matters is that one feels part of *this* community. As a result of this organic connection it follows that activities of human beings are not susceptible to abstract theorising. We cannot suggest that there is one particular form of social organisation that best fits humanity.

Conservatives again rely on empirical evidence in support of this organicist view. First, they point to the existence of distinct and separate cultures, which are usually defined by a common language. These cultures also have their own sense of community and sense of belonging. Quinton goes so far as to suggest that this is indicative of distinct national characteristics. The second empirical support is that 'Western' political models, such as liberal democracy and Marxism, have not been particularly exportable to the developing world. Where they have been exported they have often been hybridised by the local political culture and have developed into something that is quite specific to that culture.

Organicism can be seen as both a logical and metaphysical necessity, as indeed it is in Hegel's *Elements of the Philosophy of Right* (1991). It is the belief in an absolutely necessary connection to a particular community. However, we need not take such an essentialist position as Hegel. Instead a more down-to-earth position would be simply to suggest that individuals are formed within a particular culture and can do little without a connection to social networks.

What this discussion leaves us with is a sense of conservatism as being concerned with preserving and protecting particular ways of life in all their specificity and difference. This leads us to what is a central concern of conservative thought, which is the manner in which individuals are connected to the social whole. This is achieved, according to conservatives, through the institution of private property.

Owning things

It is interesting that when the discussion turns to property ownership conservative thinkers are at their most articulate and even tend towards the abstract. It is as if, in discussing ownership, they can place conservatism on firmer foundations, something, as it were, more solid on which to base a justification for the conservative disposition. Hence Scruton (2001) becomes more categorical when discussing property, or what he describes as 'the absolute and ineradicable need for private property' (p 92). We can again see a Hegelian strain in his thinking when he states:

> Ownership is the primary relation through which man and nature come together. It is therefore the first stage in the socialising of objects, and the condition of all higher institutions. It is not necessarily a product of greed or exploitation, but it is necessarily a part of the process whereby people free themselves from the power of things, transforming resistant nature into compliant image. Through property man imbues his world with will, and begins therein to discover himself as a social being. (2001, p 92)

Without property we cannot identify any object in the world as our own, and hence we have no right to use any object, nor can we expect others to allow us access to it (not that they could, of course, because they would have no rights over it either). Without rights of ownership everything is merely an object of desire. Objects without ownership can play no part in social relations: there can be no exchange, no gifts and no transfers from one person to another.

Scruton argues that if people are to become fully aware of themselves as agents who are capable of independent action within a social whole, then they need to see the world in terms of rights, responsibility and freedom. He suggests that it is 'The institution of property [that] allows them to do this' (2001, p 93). By making an object mine I can now use it for my purposes. I am able to be more active because my possibilities have been increased. But I am also given a responsibility, for I now have to determine how it can be used, whether I should share my access and so on. As Scruton states, 'Through property an object ceases to be a mere inanimate thing, and becomes instead the focus of rights and obligations' (2001, p 93). Through property ownership 'the object is lifted out of mere "thinghood" and rendered up to humanity' (Scruton, 2001, p 93). It bears the imprint of social relations and reflects back to the owner 'a picture of himself as a social being' (Scruton, 2001, p 93), as someone now with the capability of relations with others. Property ownership is therefore seen by Scruton as a primary social relation. It is what allows us access to the social world, as beings able to achieve our ends.

Having given this rather abstract justification of property ownership, Scruton then identifies the main form of property we experience. Ownership, as it were, grounds the self in the social world. As he states, instead of being at loose in the world, an individual is 'at home' (2001, p 93). He goes on:

> It is for this reason that a person's principal proprietary attitude is towards his immediate surroundings – house, room, furniture – towards those things with which he is, so to speak, mingled. It is the home,

therefore, that is the principal sphere of property, and the principal
locus of the gift. (p 93)

The most important form of property is the home, as this is the primary relation
we have with things. It is what we live within and what therefore becomes part
of us. When we own those things around us – the house and its contents – we
are better able to control our surroundings and disburse our personal and social
obligations. The family unit is where we show responsibility to others, where
our primary obligations are held and where we are most able to express our
generosity.

This suggests that Scruton sees no necessary connection between possession
and consumption. Indeed, he tries expressly to disconnect the two concepts. He
correctly states that consumption does not presuppose ownership, and would take
place even in a state of nature or communist paradise: comrades still need to eat.
Consumption can be seen as individual, as something that relates to individuals'
needs and desires. What it does not show is the social essence of property, and
accordingly these should be seen as distinct notions. What ownership does offer is
stability: 'The important aspect of property is its stable aspect, in which ownership
is conceived as permanent or semi-permanent. For the full fruition of the sense of
property there must be permanent objects of possession' (Scruton, 2001, p 94).

The linkage between ownership and home and household is clearly important
to conservatives. Home is where private property becomes something shared.
It is where things are simply *ours*. Scruton states that 'It is for this reason that
conservatives have seen the family and private property as institutions which
stand or fall together. The family has its life in the home, and the home demands
property for its establishment' (2001, p 94). Importantly, this is not merely some
historical accident, or just, as Marxists would have it, the model of the bourgeois
family imposed on society as a whole. As Scruton is keen to ask, where and when,
outside socialist and utopian futurist fictions, has there been the non-bourgeois
family? Accordingly, he argues that property rights are as important to working-
class families in council housing as they are to the middle classes. Property is a
particular form of right and hence 'the occupancy of a council flat is a property
right … it enables the proletarian family to accumulate goods and gadgetry … in
a manner which changes the aspect of the home' (2001, p 95). Council housing
is determined by property relations, and the rights and obligations involved offer
possibilities which convert space into a home.

This link to council housing shows that the conservative argument for property
rights is not specific to a particular set of legal relations, but rather relates to
the manner in which certain social relations can allow for the extensive use of
things by establishing rights and duties on us. These social relations can be made
manifest in different customary and legal ways which are themselves dependent
on particular cultural conditions. In Britain and the US these cultural conditions
have created a dichotomy between owning and renting, a situation which need
not pertain elsewhere.

Scruton's position is supported by Quinton (1993), who stresses the importance of property as a means of stabilising societies. Similarly, he too links ownership to the family, in that property allows family members to look after themselves. He also concurs with Scruton by suggesting that conservatives believe there is no plausible alternative to the family.

But this is, of course, a position that can be criticised, both in the abstract and because of the effects of policies such as the RTB. I wish here to restrict the criticisms to the more abstract arguments, relying particularly on the critique of Honderich (1990). His view is important in that he takes what could be called the 'standard' critique of rights, which differentiates between freedom and capability. We need to distinguish between those who have the resources as well as the freedom to act, and those who merely have the latter. In consequence, Honderich argues that property ownership merely favours one particular class. He states that 'the conservative society ... enlarges the total of what is distributed according to the ability to pay and decreases the total of what is distributed according to need' (1990, p 89). He sees property ownership as a zero-sum game, where allowing the few to gain more deprives the majority from realising their desires. He suggests that 'the conservative desire and strategy to increase to a limited extent the number of holders of some small amount of property, notably a home or a few shares' does not carry 'the great benefits of other amounts and forms of property' (1990, p 93) . Owner occupation does not, Honderich seems to believe, allow these individuals to accumulate capital, and they are therefore not part of the property-owning class in the classical Marxist sense.

This is, of course, a fairly traditional argument used by opponents of home ownership. They seek to differentiate between different types of ownership and thus to suggest that home owners are in some way being deluded. This view has been justifiably criticised by libertarian and anarchist writers such as Turner (1976) and Ward (1985). What the argument neglects is the significance of what Honderich rather patronisingly refers to as a 'small amount of property' to the individuals themselves. The importance of property is not related to consumption or to accumulation, but to what it allows individuals to do. It allows us protection; to show and receive care; to be close with those we love; and to show reciprocity and offer support to those significant to us.

Conservatives would argue that the importance of extending home ownership is that it extends a personal relation into a socially significant one. Property ownership offers the most effective means for institutionalising privacy: it protects private relations and does this through the socialisation of key relations, whereby others recognise our right to exclusive use.

But this does not answer Honderich's criticism of the exclusive nature of ownership, whereby the holdings of a minority deprive access to it by the majority. But when we start to consider what it is that Conservative governments did in Britain in the late 20th century, we see that they have actually attempted to do the opposite. Their policies towards owner occupation have not been about exclusion but about distribution, with extending ownership further. As Scruton (2001, p 95) has suggested:

> the essential connection between household and family is undeniable. It follows that conservatives must be concerned with the distribution of property, and not only its accumulation. Given their belief in the political importance of the family, and their reliance on family loyalties in forming respect towards an established political order, they must desire the distribution of property through all classes of society, in accordance with whatever conception of household might be generic to each of them.

What concerns conservatives is the extension of ownership, and this is why the RTB is a policy of such elemental importance, as well as being so emblematic of the conservative disposition.

But before moving on to consider the RTB in detail, there is a further concept I wish to explore. We have defined conservatism and linked it to ownership. However, what is also important about the conservative disposition is the manner in which we are able to use our dwelling and make of it what we want. The dwelling gives us privacy and we seek to maintain this. We achieve this through the use of our own income. We are accordingly able to show both an independence from others and a capability through the manner in which we use our own resources within and for our own dwelling.

Our discussion therefore shifts onto more practical ground. We move away from political theory and towards the way in which we use the resources at our disposal. One reason for this discussion is to tackle head on one of the key criticisms of the RTB, namely that it is merely an opportunistic policy based on financial inducements. I want to show how, as part of our ordinary existence, we link the financial and the existential – the asset and the use – into a cohesive whole. Like the desire to own property, this too can be seen as part of the conservative disposition.

Using things

In normal times[6] our continued relation with the financing of our dwelling, despite its importance, tends to be rather distant. Practically it is most likely that we make payments by a direct debit through our bank, and the only contact we have from our lender is through an annual statement of what we have paid and what we still owe. Of course, there are other issues we need to attend to, such as paying bills and annual insurance renewals. We tend to deal with these in ways that are formal, by letter and through arrangements with banks again. If we are particularly modern, we might now make some of these arrangements online.

But what there is not is any direct contact with financial institutions. There is very little face-to-face contact after the initial mortgage is negotiated and agreed.

We might, from time to time, change our mortgage, set up a new fixed-rate arrangement, or change our energy supplier, but this is all done through formal administrative procedures. There is nothing that is intimate or close, and this applies even though finance is something we might treat as private and confidential. We exclude others not to preserve our intimacy, but solely because we wish no one else to be involved.

This, however, is exactly how we wish the relationship over housing finance to be and precisely as it should be. We want a high degree of formality as this is more likely to ensure the security of our assets. But we have next to no expectations of our lender other than that they treat us with competence, fairness and honesty. We want, and need, to have no further relationship with our mortgage lender or electricity supplier. We require a means to contact them and some means of redress if they fail in their obligations. We expect clarity in terms of what we will be, and have been, charged and that the service they are contracted to provide will be delivered. Yet we expect no day-to-day contact and so they remain distant. We continue to live in the dwelling, the lights come on, water comes out of the taps and the bins are emptied. All we need do is pay the bills.

And as long as we maintain the payments and pay our bills, we will not be bothered. The cycles go on; there is a regularity in terms of the relationship with these agencies. We make our regular payments and in return we can continue on with our lives free from interference. Of course, mortgage lenders and energy companies can influence what we do, most particularly if prices change. If mortgage payments or energy bills increase we might have to alter our behaviour. But despite this, the relationship with these bodies is a formal one. These companies do not seek to improve us or control us. They merely wish us to pay our bills on time. This is the main condition of the relationship: that we pay what we owe and in return they supply us with a service. All our mortgage lender is interested in is the contractual relationship between us and they are content to leave us alone. We can only be identified by a code or reference number, and despite attempts to personalise their service and the importance of good manners, we expect and respect this level of formality which we see as guaranteeing a degree of competence and certainty.

But these formal relations exist to provide us with something that is very intimate. The finance supports the activity of dwelling, whereby we are able to sustain, care and protect ourselves and those close to us. Indeed, our dwelling – the place where we live – is itself something that is very close to us. We operate within it. It wraps us up and encloses us. The dwelling allows us to include those we love and to exclude all others. It acts as a barrier that is physical and psychological. We are close to it because of what it allows us to do and what it prevents, particularly ingress of the unwanted, but also because of what it means to us. It is our personal place, where we can care and share without inhibition (King, 2004a; 2005; 2008).

The virtue of our private dwelling is that it allows us to be secure and complacent about our surroundings and our place in the world. We might see complacency as a vice, as where we ignore the world around us, or where we do not face up to the world as it is, but rather seek to take things only on our terms. Yet this is precisely why dwelling is so significant to us. We need some place where we can be free of the expectations of others and where we relax and act only with regard to our intimates. The privacy and security of private dwelling, which prevents unwanted others from impinging upon us, allows for this complacency (King, 2003; 2005; 2008). This sense of private dwelling, of course, is something shared by most households.

What private dwelling provides us with is *regularity* and this returns us to the financial basis of our housing. Our financial affairs may be formal and perhaps somewhat distant, but they are cyclical and are based on a regularity of actions and commitments. These formal relations provide us with patterns of consistency which allow only for slow and predictable change. This allows us to plan, but also to continue on within our complacency. Once we have set up our financial relations – our standing orders, so to speak – we need not do much more. We can run on autopilot without worrying about dramatic changes and whether we can maintain our lifestyle. If we wish to take risks we can do and we will have a base from which to leap. The stability of our base allows us to change and commit to new opportunities in a manner that would not be possible were the stability not present beneath us. But, because of that support, we need not take the risk.

When we talk of regularity we think of precise intervals and of repetition. 'Regularity', of course, is the noun of 'regular', which we can see as referring to what is normal, customary, usual and expected. It is where processes develop according to a uniform principle, or occur at fixed or pre-arranged intervals. When things are regular they follow a set rule or practice.

To be regular is to be a creature of habit, one who is consistent and who follows established patterns of behaviour. We see such people as dependable and efficient and who perhaps have a balanced view of their place in the world. They may be somewhat formal, but this can be a virtue when dealing with finance or impersonal relations. But particularly important for our discussion here is the sense that regularity has of depending on the expected and what is normal. If we can establish regularity there are no surprises, but rather patterns and predictability. This allows us to feel secure and stable, that we are not in a precarious position or under threat. We can take our situation for granted in the belief that contingencies are taken care of. There is a sense in which we can accept our environment and our place in it and feel that we belong (King, 2008). We do not have to strive for our ends, but feel that we are close to them. It is where we are comfortable, not just in the material sense, but in the existential sense of knowing our place within the world (King, 2005). Regularity, therefore, allows for the existential and the financial to be brought together.

I wish to refer to this manner in which we can underpin the existential, and create regularity, as *really private finance*.[7] I shall use the term to relate to the level of activity that centres on individual decision making and individual relationships concerning housing. It is a term that need not be reserved for housing, although the nature of housing is such that there is always likely to be a direct financial relationship with bodies external to the household, unlike those goods that are provided by the state free of charge, such as education and health care.

But I also want to use the term 'really private finance' precisely because not all the cost of housing, for some households at least, is met from their own resources. Housing is open to public policy intervention and government provides finance to support the production and consumption of housing. So housing finance is an arena of government action and this alters the nature of private activity (King, 2009). The issue of public finance is therefore an important one.

Accordingly, there is a more knowing and ironic meaning to the use of the term 'really private finance' and in particular the word 'really'. This is because of the importance to housing, and public provision in particular, of what has become known as *private finance*. Since the end of the 1980s, successive governments have engineered a situation where new social provision can only be built with a significant private contribution. Public grants are limited to a fixed proportion of the capital cost and the residue must be raised by private borrowing. In addition, since 1990, over a million council dwellings have been transferred to housing associations, meaning that private finance is also now used to improve and maintain the stock.

Government housing policy depends on private finance and the levels of activity could not be maintained without it. Private finance is used to offset public expenditure and is managed in such a way that the government retains control over systems whilst minimising its financial liabilities. The government seeks to pass the risk on to private institutions in return for a reasonable rate of return. But the government still maintains bureaucratic control over the housing (King, 2009).

What this means is that what we have come to refer to as private finance is actually glaringly *public*. The term 'private finance' is always used in relation to public policy and to public projects. It is a means of funding state-sponsored projects without the government having to commit to the expenditure itself. Hence we have seen an increasing use of the so-called *Private Finance Initiative* (PFI) as a means of funding public projects through the private sector and paying for these through long-term revenue funding.

Private finance is used to fund public projects and it is being defined by the government as a means of meeting its policy objectives. Indeed, as was shown recently by the failure of Metronet, a PFI company involved in improving the London Underground, the government has had to underwrite these activities. It is simply unrealistic for large-scale public infrastructure such as the capital's underground system to fail as a result of the collapse of a particular funding mechanism. In 2009 the British government had to intervene and provide funding for several PFI projects that were struggling to achieve the requisite private funding. Accordingly, we now have the thoroughgoing absurdity of a public-funded Private Finance Initiative. This shows that what we take to be private is not *really* that at all.

Private finance is controlled by the government and has a specific public function. It has developed as a top-down process to suit government priorities, particularly the need to control public expenditure whilst increasing or maintaining outputs. Private finance has been initiated, therefore, out of public processes to achieve public ends, and has not arisen out of the operation of private organisations or through spontaneous actions. So 'private finance' is actually a public policy mechanism. We might say, therefore, that it is somewhat *unreal*.

In contrast, really private finance is about what individuals do with their own money, in their own time, to meet their own ends. We might say that it is *properly* private, in that it is not controlled by anyone other than the individual that owns it.[8] It is the use of finance for private purposes, and it very much pre-dates the use of private finance as a policy mechanism. Really private finance should be seen as concerned with bottom-up processes, initiated by individual households taking decisions based on the circumstances they find themselves in. Really private finance is about how we use our own money to meet our own needs, wants and aspirations. Quite clearly these actions can have a public impact in aggregate, and the government can seek to use fiscal and monetary policy to try to affect the behaviour of individuals. But the government does not initiate these actions, and they do not arise out of the government's purposes. Governments may involve themselves in income maintenance and, of course, they tax the income of individuals. But it is not generally seen as the role of government to direct the expenditure of individuals. Indeed, modern governments do not see it as their role to ensure income equality, even if they might seek to ensure a minimum income.

Generally speaking, we are assumed to be able to use our income as we please, and this is the sense in which I use the term 'really private finance'. How we use our income is no concern of anyone but ourselves. The outcomes of this use are our problem and our responsibility. Any benefit that accrues is ours, and any loss falls on us too. What we are concerned with, therefore, is those decisions we make and which only we can properly make (and still have income to control). Really private finance is about how we use our resources for our purposes, on the basis of our definition of these purposes and in our own time and in our own way.

What concerns me here is not how we gain the income, but how we use what we have. So once an individual is given income support through a government scheme, it becomes theirs and is really private. The government recognises this basic principle through the use of income maintenance schemes rather than through the use of food and clothing vouchers. Interestingly, it is now UK government policy to make Housing Benefit payments directly to claimants rather than allowing the subsidy to be paid to their landlord. The justification for this change is the need to build personal responsibility by ensuring that tenants pay their own rent. They should be able to manage their own responsibilities and this can be done through the control over a personal income as is the case for those individuals who earn their own income (DWP, 2002). The drift in welfare policy appears to be moving towards personal responsibility and the idea, therefore, that we all have access to really private finance.

For the majority of households this is already the case in that what we achieve is through the use of our own income on the basis of the plans we have devised and tried to implement. This is not a perfect situation, in that there may be a considerable gap between our aspirations and our achievements. But, nevertheless, what we do achieve is the result of our own initiative.

The importance of the concept of really private finance, though, is more significant than as merely a critique of government housing and welfare policies. The concept, I believe, is very important in teasing out the manner in which we can and do use our housing and the manner in which we want or aspire to do so. The concept helps us get to the heart of the relationship between our dwelling and ourselves as thinking, acting beings who are capable of setting goals and deciding on a means of achieving them.

Really private finance helps clarify for us the possibilities and limits that surround us in the dwelling. It demonstrates to us what we can and cannot do. By putting an emphasis both on our own resources and what we wish to use them for it brings into clear focus what we are able to do with the dwelling, and what dwelling allows us to do. It enables us to state what it is that we must do for ourselves and what cannot be done by anyone but ourselves. Really private finance, being concerned with the use of our resources within the sphere of our own private actions, focuses down on our responsibilities and the limitations this may place on us. It takes as a given that we have responsibilities for our family and the upkeep of the dwelling itself and helps to demonstrate the centrality of these relations.

But it also shows that the most private sphere is linked into markets and the wider social whole, even up to the global level. Our income − *our* really private finance − is derived from the external world of employment and government policy and practice. We are therefore at the mercy of the external world to some extent. We may have some insulation from external influence because of our savings and the assets we hold, or because we can rely on the resources of others, such as our parents. Alternatively, we might have exactly the right circumstances for particular market conditions, for instance, a small mortgage relative to the value of our house and income, and so we are not affected markedly once housing markets decline. But whatever the specific case, the insulation we might have is never total, and sooner or later we will have to face up to the limitations of market conditions and government action.

An appreciation of our own resources and the expectations we have of them and of our dwelling environment might help us to understand why we do not need intervention when we are comfortable, but also what intervention is for once we, or others, have too few resources. This, at one level, might appear to be an obvious point − rich people can look after themselves, but poor people cannot − yet the reality is rather more complex, as we can quite readily see when we begin to consider not just income levels but the issues of commitments and expectations: do we expect our situation to improve or worsen, and what leeway do we have to cope if it worsens? Is our family increasing in size – more mouths to feed – or decreasing, because our children are leaving home? Can we reasonably expect our income to rise over time and so might we be able to afford a bigger mortgage? Is there a reasonable prospect of house price inflation? What are our priorities and interests regarding how we live? How capable are we of deciding our own affairs, and what happens if – or when – this changes?

This combination of income, aspirations, expectations and decision-making capability starts to show the complexity of our housing situation and why it is not simply sufficient to concentrate on one factor such as income. In other words, it properly personalises the relationship between finance and housing in a manner that goes beyond the generalities normally associated with the subject of housing finance. It stresses that we do not merely respond to financial stimuli.

The concept of really private finance is important in that it starts to regulate and determine the role of other agencies we relate to, and consequently puts the work of these agencies into some perspective. By making clear what opportunities and limits there are to our own income, choices and aspirations, it questions what role government and other agencies might have. It helps to state what government and other agencies cannot and must not do if they are to allow us to dwell privately, and what forms of intervention are legitimate. By stating the proper relations between private dwelling and finance – by making clear what is *really private* – we can start to see what we can do for ourselves and so where the potential gaps are. But importantly, the determination of what is legitimate and where the limits are is not formed entirely externally, but as a result of the relationship between our housing and our income, current circumstances and aspirations. The concept of 'really private finance', therefore, can provide us with a helpful bottom-up approach to understanding the complexities of dwelling as lived experience.

We need to appreciate that finance may not be at the heart of our decision making. We might not make a decision solely on financial grounds, but rather rely on finance as the enabler or facilitator of our needs and aspirations. It is all too easy for those whose primary interest is finance to forget that housing finance is a means and not an end in itself (King, 2009). It might be that financial considerations impinge only at certain times. Obviously this would be when we need to buy or sell a dwelling, but it will also be when housing markets are in recession and we become anxious about the value of our dwelling or increases in our housing costs. It is clear that if we are in debt and struggling to repay our mortgage, then housing finance will loom very large in our consciousness. But then not all of us will react in the same manner: some people may be more sanguine about debt than others, and see it as a sustainable position. Others might hide from the issue and refuse to deal with it, on the basis that something might turn up or that they may never have to face the problem.[9] So some people may not even consider finance – their mortgage or rent arrears – even when they clearly ought to.

We perhaps see finance as something of a mystery, as something we only use when we have to. Most of us, most of the time, are sufficiently comfortable that we have a considerable margin, which allows us to ignore finance, or rather to take it for granted. We do not need to understand how financial markets work and unless we are faced with a crisis we do not even notice how ignorant we are. All we need to be aware of is how much we are paying and for how long.

But I do not see this as financial incompetence or ignorance. It is not that we do not understand something important. Instead it is a case of the complacency that comes from regularity. We have made our payments consistently and see no reason why we will not continue to do so into the future. We do not believe we have anything to worry about because we feel, based on our experience, that our housing is affordable. We expect that we can carry on as before and that the financial arrangements will be consistent and predictable. When this situation alters so will our perception of housing finance. This might lead us to suggest that we should all become 'financial experts' once we are faced with a threat to our complacency. The near collapse of world financial markets and the steep decline in house prices in 2008 and onwards has heightened our awareness of housing finance to the extent that US mortgage institutions like Fannie Mae and Freddie Mac feature on the UK national news. When house prices were rising and households felt more affluent, they had no need to understand the workings of mortgage lenders and where they sourced their finance and what the implications were. But now, after the failure of Northern Rock, this has become a very important political issue.

By focusing on the personal level we can start to appreciate the impact of changes at the macro-level and the manner in which we might or might not respond at the micro-level. If we have a reasonable income and a relatively small mortgage compared to the value of our dwelling we might not alter our behaviour. But if we have just bought a property and mortgaged ourselves up to the limit in the expectation that the good times would continue, we might have to drastically reduce our discretionary expenditure and may well fear that our housing will become unaffordable, even though we cannot afford to sell the house because of the loss we would incur.

This does not mean that finance is everything, however, even as we find ourselves in difficulties. As Turner (1976) has argued, we need to differentiate between the economic and human values of housing. We need to remember that housing has an existential significance, it binds us to our environment and allows us to fulfil our ends, and it can do this without regard to the material value of the dwelling, or even, Turner argues, without necessarily any direct correlation to material standards and amenities.

A dwelling still fulfils the same function for us as needful human beings whether it is valued at £180,000 or falls to £150,000. We can use it in the same manner on a day-to-day basis. Indeed, even if we are in mortgage arrears the dwelling still continues to shelter and protect us. Of course, it will not continue to do so indefinitely and we will be forced to act to remedy the situation, but this does not alter the basic qualities offered by the dwelling.

So Turner argues for a distinction between the existential and economic values of the dwelling. However, there is a connection between the existential and the economic. Indeed, the fact that we have to pay for the dwelling demonstrates this link at the most basic level. However, this connection is not necessarily straightforward or simple to understand. We might see the existential and economic as two sides of the same coin. It is precisely the virtue of the concept of really private finance, which connects use and expectations with resources and so links the existential and economic into one practical conception, that allows us to make sense of this connection. What really private finance allows is for both the connection *and* distinction between the activity of dwelling and its material value, both as an object in itself and its economic significance as an object connected to the external world.

The determining factor in really private finance is personal decision making, or, rather, how our personal decision making relates to general external factors. The importance of housing finance to us is, to a considerable extent, dependent upon our actions. We are, of course, affected by external factors, such as global markets and government action, and we can have little control over these. But, we need to remember that the operation of these external factors is nearly always general. Changes in market conditions are not directed at particular individuals or groups, but have their effect because of the particular situation that an individual or group finds themself in. Again, even though government action might be more targeted than market activity, it is still general and its impact dependent on the specific situation of the individual or group. So, markets and governments act in a general way and how they impact is dependent on the specific situations in which individuals find themselves. These situations derive from the actions individuals have taken and the choices they have made.

So, for example, a household might have mortgaged themselves to the hilt and left themselves with no leeway if interest rates rise. Another household might have been cautious and maintained a relatively small mortgage. In this way these households are either prepared or unprepared to meet changes over which they have no control, such as an economic downturn, higher interest rates, stagnant real-term income growth and so on. We may, indeed, see these latter issues as the real problems, and they will, indeed, cause considerable difficulties to some households. Yet this does not detract from the overall point that an individual household's situation is dependent on the choices they have made in terms of house purchase. We are therefore always in part culpable in terms of what happens to us.

It might be argued that some households have no alternative. The shortage of available dwellings to rent, and their inability to access social housing, means that some households have no alternative but to buy a property and to do this they borrow heavily and, perhaps in hindsight, recklessly. This being so, how can they be held responsible for changes in housing markets which make their situation unsustainable? Any answer to this question will have the tendency to sound either glib or unsympathetic, or perhaps even both. However, this situation is precisely why an understanding of really private finance is so important. No one who purchases a dwelling, regardless of the pressure they feel they are facing, can reasonably have done so under actual duress. Households are not forced to buy any particular dwelling. However, it is doubtless the case that some households feel that they have no alternative but to buy an expensive dwelling in London. Yet, most people *need not* live in London, but do so because of family connection, employment or other lifestyle reasons. These are all entirely valid on their own terms, and it would be impertinent for anyone to question them, but it does not mean that the household is *forced* to stay in the most expensive city in the country.

What is at the heart of the problem is that individuals believe that they should be able to live where they please and that they should be able to do so as owner-occupiers. They have certain expectations which motivate their behaviour, and which preclude them from taking other decisions, such as finding a job and renting a flat in Newcastle. No one, of course, can or should be forced into doing this. However, it also follows that those who do not take this course of action open themselves up to a series of consequences which are entirely predictable. Accordingly, we can conclude that they are responsible for their predicament. This does not mean that many households might not be facing considerable hardship and anxiety. However, it does not follow that anyone but themselves should bear the consequences of their decisions.

Indeed, the way in which we expect the government to act serves to reinforce this understanding that our predicament is self-made. We might accept that bank deposits should be guaranteed by the government, at least up to a certain amount,[10] but we do not believe that it should guarantee the value of our house. Neither do we think that it is improper for a lender to seek repossession if we default on the mortgage. Whilst we would not want this action taken against ourselves or those we know, or even enjoy the prospect of it happening to anyone, we can see that it is a necessary part of how markets work. We realise what the consequences would be if there was no sanction against mortgage defaulters.

In a housing recession we might expect the government to act and use fiscal and monetary policy to effect a recovery in housing markets. We might also accept that there may be the need for emergency measures in some extreme circumstances. But what we do not expect is for the government to assist in individual cases. Instead, like much of government action, the intervention should be general rather than case-by-case intervention.

An individual is presumed to be in control of their finances and to be competent to pay their bills and meet their responsibilities. They are deemed able to make choices and to be aware of the consequences. We assume a degree of personal responsibility and culpability on the part of individuals, and consequently we believe that they must bear at least some of the responsibility for their financial difficulties, and this applies even when we might agree that the person has really just been unlucky and has done very little wrong, for example, those who chose to buy an expensive house just as the market was turning. Households can suffer from bad luck, but this does not mean that they should be cushioned from the impact of their choices. The problem is that we cannot, or find it very difficult to, separate out the ill luck from the bad decision, and these from the deliberate act of omission or reckless decision. We also might believe that providing for these cases will encourage recklessness and acts of omission (King, 2000).

But perhaps a more pertinent reason is that we just do not believe it is anyone else's business to interfere in the private affairs of an individual. We have taken a decision based not on the general good, but on our own interests. This is in itself perfectly normal. However, it does mean that we cannot expect society to support us. We do not seek to take property off those who are just lucky or have shown good judgement (or at least not most of it), and we also do not feel we should bale out those who are unlucky or have shown poor judgement. This is simply taken as a proper consequence of personal decision making.

For government to actually deal with ill luck would involve a tremendous amount of intervention and arbitrary assumptions on what constitutes good and bad luck, and what is the legitimate scope for personal decision making. We can see a link here with Nozick's thought experiment on perfect equality, his 'Wilt Chamberlain' case, where government has to reallocate income even though all transfers have been voluntary (Nozick, 1974). Nozick describes a hypothetical society of perfect income equality. However, many individuals are prepared to pay a voluntary premium to watch a particularly talented basketball player, Wilt Chamberlain. At the end of the basketball season Chamberlain has a considerably higher income than the rest of the society, but this has arisen entirely out of voluntary actions taken by individuals aware of what they were doing. Nozick argues that income equality could only be maintained by considerable and continuous intervention by the government that runs counter to the voluntary decisions of individuals within the society who have taken great pleasure in watching an exceptional sportsperson.

Likewise for the government to involve itself in dealing with individual cases of ill luck would involve an absurd and impractical level of intervention and forced transfers. It would effectively involve the nationalisation of the housing stock and its general allocation through some central and uniform standard procedure.

But it would also exonerate any individual of any culpability for the situation they find themself in and create a considerable moral hazard, whereby the incidence of the undesired outcome would increase. If we were aware that we would not bear the consequences of our action we might well behave in an irresponsible and arbitrary manner. The fact that we know we will have to bear the consequences of our actions is an important element in making rational decisions. Without personal responsibility we could act with impunity and effectively become infantilised.

Conclusions

So having the control over our own money, and recognising that we should have, alters the manner in which we relate to our dwelling and to the wider world. The concept of really private finance therefore deals not just with the use we make of our dwelling, but the manner in which we are responsible for both the dwelling and what it contains. It is this sense of bringing use and responsibility together that brings us to property ownership and the RTB in particular. Really private finance clearly shows a concern for the extrinsic, for the surface of things. It concerns how we use our dwelling and what our expectations are for ourselves and those close to us. It shows that what matters is not the control over the dwelling itself, but what the control allows. Rights over property allow us to exercise a degree of control and so match our income with our expectations and aspirations. In turn, this allows us to keep things close and to better control our environment.

The concept of really private finance also shows that our dwelling depends on personal responsibility. So, linking the concept to Scruton (2001) and his justification of ownership as being necessary for social relations, we can suggest that ownership brings with it a responsibility which itself embeds social relations. This responsibility, which at times might be onerous, is an enabling of the social. And crucially, this responsibility depends upon our ability to control the private realm and to marshal our resources to the fulfilment of our chosen ends.

Yet this concern for really private finance shows that being private is not the same as being isolated. Indeed, it can be said to show the opposite, that we are made *socially* responsible through the concern we have to show for ourselves and our loved ones. We are taking care of what is close to us and having to use the resources around us to achieve and maintain this. It is this insight that takes us beyond the purely financial and on to the use we can put our dwelling to. It also starts to show that our concern is not to attain a dwelling but to sustain it so that we can use it. A dwelling is a means to an end, and this means that the rights over it must be seen in the same way. Rights allow us to use the dwelling as we will, and this is why they are important.

Connecting this discussion to the RTB means that we should look to what the RTB does, to what it facilitates. This necessitates a disaggregated view of the policy, so that we do not concentrate on numbers sold or shifts in the stock of dwellings, but rather that we focus on what the RTB allowed individual households to do. The RTB connected with aspiration and altered expectations. It allowed people the perception and reality of greater control and to feel that they were achieving an independence, of becoming really private. But in doing so, they became part of some bigger whole through the responsibilities that their new rights brought with them.

Notes

[1] The difference between political culture in England and Scotland and Wales is an important but rather complex issue. Clearly we can suggest that both Scotland and Wales are less conservative and have been more amenable to the Labour Party and socialist ideas. However, the size of England within the UK – and the Conservative voting majority for much of the 20th century – has meant that conservatism has dominated electorally. Where the controversy enters is whether we see that there has been a cultural domination to go alongside the electoral and political. This is an issue I engage with later in this chapter, but time and space does not allow for the full answer that this question deserves.

[2] By this I mean that the culture has a particular conservative tenor. This need not mean that all parts of it, or all individuals subscribing to that culture, are themselves conservative.

[3] Indeed, Kirk does not depend on political thought and thinkers for his discussion, preferring to rely on writers like Fennimore Cooper, Macaulay, Carlyle, Scott and Eliot.

[4] But we should also note that Scruton's language, in all its elegance, is not that of the saloon bar. He is very far from the inarticulate conservative.

[5] There is an interesting link here with the libertarianism of Robert Nozick (1974), who argued that it was illegitimate to use one person for the benefit of another. However, the linkage is limited in that Nozick went on to use this principle to suggest that there was no social good, merely individual goods over which no one else had any rights.

[6] At the time of writing (late 2008–early 2009) the world of finance is anything but normal. However, my aim here is to show how we do operate in the usual situation of economic stability, which, after all, was the state in which most of us, including RTB households, have taken our major financial decisions.

[7] It has been pointed out to me that this phrase resonates with 'really existing socialism' and so might be seen to have a rather defensive quality to it, as in 'never mind what it is meant to be in theory this is what it actually is in practice'. I must admit that I find this connection amusing, but it was not deliberate. My use of the word 'really' here is to draw attention to the fact that what is commonly called 'private finance' is actually a creation of public policy and has little to do with the actions of private – that is, not government-sponsored – activity.

[8] An alternative to 'really private finance' might have been 'personal finance', but this carries with it a particular link to financial services (banking, insurance, pensions and so on) and so did not really create the right sort of associations. Personal finance can be seen to be about relations with others, and so has become used in a particular technical way, whereas I am trying here to develop the sense of how we decide to use our own resources on our own terms.

[9] I deal with this issue of hiding from responsibility in my book *In Dwelling* (King, 2008).

[10] In October 2008 the UK government increased its savings guarantee from £35,000 to £50,000, whilst several European governments offered 100% guarantees.

What Mrs Thatcher did

Introduction

One of the fascinating aspects of Conservative Party thinking in the mid- to late 1970s was its intellectual robustness and utter self-confidence. The Conservatives were sure that they were moving with the grain of the British people. When we read the policy documents of the years between Mrs Thatcher's election as leader in 1975 and the 1979 election there is a definite sense of purpose, of a political party with a mission. This mission was no less than the transformation of the country and the defeat of socialism. In this regard, Mrs Thatcher may have been correct to portray herself as a 'conservative revolutionary' (Green, 2006). She saw an enemy and set out to defeat it. What is more, she knew what weapons to use and was confident that she could win.

Of course, political documents do not usually contain much in the way of doubt and ambiguity. Political parties like to portray things in straightforward terms – good versus bad, 'Axis of Evil' and so on – and do not wish to show that their position is actually hedged with caveats and compromise. Yet, the vision that the Conservatives sought to put across after 1975 was a strident and confident one.

This is the context in which we ought to view the Right to Buy (RTB): an intellectually confident party, firm in the belief that history, and the British people, was on their side, seeking to transform what they saw as an ossified and derelict state which was dragging the British people down into mediocrity. They knew they were facing an intellectually bankrupt and failing government and that they could provide a real and vital alternative. The RTB was meant to be transformative and to really stir things up.

In this chapter I want to consider what the Conservatives actually did – what the policy was and how it worked – but to do so through the lens of intention. Discussions of policy can be descriptive, but what I seek to do here is to show what was meant by the RTB. Accordingly, I wish to consider the RTB on its own terms, as something that an avowedly radical, perhaps even revolutionary, government felt was right. This, I believe, is one aspect of the RTB that is seldom considered. As I have stated, there is a marked reluctance to take conservative ideas seriously, and never on their own terms. The RTB is dealt with in terms of other tenures and through the lens of its opponents. The mistake has been to underestimate the meaning of the RTB through concentrating mainly on its effects on other sectors.

There are three things, in particular, that I wish to consider in this chapter. First, I want to look at the general issue of whether we should take ideas at face value, and if it is ever appropriate to question the motives of politicians. My reason for doing this is that I wish to challenge those who argue that only one side in any debate is virtuous. It is all too easy to impugn the motives of our opponents as a simplistic way of trying to defeat them. But what if they actually mean it honestly and sincerely, just like we do? This, I believe, alters the tenor of the debate on a controversial policy such as the RTB. Having done this, I then go on to look at the underpinning reasons why the policy was introduced: what did Mrs Thatcher and the Conservatives mean to do with the RTB? The third part of the chapter will then describe what the RTB actually involved. My aim here is to offer an outline of what the policy consisted of and how it has changed over time. There is a considerable literature on this, as well as explanatory leaflets and websites, and the basic nature of the policy is well known. So my aim in this last section is indeed descriptive. I see the discussions on motive and meaning as more important and distinctive, as are those which follow in subsequent chapters on the impact of the RTB, the past and current criticisms of it, and the more general lessons we can learn.

But did she mean it?

It is all too easy to ascribe particular motivations to others, to assume that they act from some ulterior motive, from some hidden or unspoken agenda which they then ruthlessly seek to prosecute whilst cynically and calculatingly trying to deny anything but their moral rectitude. It is easy to argue that President Bush went to war in Iraq in 2003 for oil or to accommodate the interests of big business (Klein, 2007). Those we disagree with always act for inglorious and selfish motives, just as we are always moral and selfless. Arguing in this manner is easy and allows for simple conclusions that others can understand and appreciate. This is why people read writers like Naomi Klein: she offers clear-cut answers to complex and hitherto intractable problems, and does so by attributing simplistic moral causation to the actions of people and organisations. She identifies the 'good guys' and the 'bad guys', those who act for selfish motives and those who act for the common good.

But, we might actually argue that this ascription of motivation actually says more about the critic than those being criticised. The critic needs to fit actions into their predetermined position. They see the world in a particular manner and insist that all actions subscribe to this position and, accordingly, actions gain their signification in terms of the prejudice of the critic. The result is a neat, simple and contained position that appears to offer a complete explanation of the phenomena in question.

The problem, however, is that such explanations are almost invariably flawed, and often downright wrong. This is because no attempt has been made to understand motivations on any other terms but those of the critic. Instead phenomena are placed in preformed categories so as to conform to an already existing position. No real thought is involved because the conclusion was reached before the analysis.

The same prejudging occurs with the RTB. Assumptions are made about its purpose, and motivations are ascribed to the Conservative government that introduced it. Yet in the literature there is little attempt to look at what Mrs Thatcher and her colleagues actually intended, or said they wanted to achieve. Instead their actions are judged according to preconceived notions about the role of social housing, owner occupation and the legitimacy of conservatism.

One question we must always ask critics (and indeed ourselves) when they (and we) are ascribing motives to others, is whether they (we) too act according to the same base motivation. If we see others as cynical, is that how we act as well? Do we too have a hidden agenda and seek to manipulate others to achieve it? Do we always put our own interests above others'? And if we answer 'no' to these questions – as I hope we would – why should we assume others act in that manner just because we disapprove of their politics and do not agree with what they seek to achieve from political action and public policy?

Most critics of Thatcherism would find the accusation that they are self-seeking and cynical as offensive, and in most cases they would be right to be offended. But this does not prevent them from ascribing simplistic motivations to Thatcher and her government. And we only need spend a few minutes reading critics from the right to see the motives of left-of-centre politicians likewise being impugned.[1]

If we wish our arguments to be taken as honest and well-meant, it behoves us to treat the arguments and intentions of others in a like manner. The proper and fair-minded way to proceed, therefore, is to take intentions at face value and only argue otherwise if there is some prima facie reason to do so. We should assume that others are sincere and that they mean what they say. We might see certain arguments as wrong-headed and even dangerous; we might see these people as being deluded. Yet we should also accept these statements and arguments as the legitimate basis for action. President Bush might have been wrong about going to war in Iraq, but we should not doubt the sincerity of his reasons for doing so.

What this means for the RTB is that we can never properly understand it by placing a preformed template on it, or by casting our own prejudices onto the actions of others. Rather we need to look at what the Conservatives actually intended for the RTB, what it was actually meant to achieve, why it was pursued in the manner it was, what its intended benefits were and what was felt to be wrong with the status quo. In short, we need to assume the sincerity of those who proposed and introduced the RTB and to take their position seriously. As well as looking at the policy of the RTB, we should consider the ideas and intentions behind the policy. It is my belief that we need to understand it on its own terms rather than simply trying to fit it into a pre-existing template.

Politics is undoubtedly a cynical business and one that involves a considerable degree of calculation and compromise. Politicians do not adopt pure ideas and apply them, but tend to pick and choose according to circumstance and then mould these ideas and arguments to suit their intentions. Both Thatcher and Reagan railed against 'big government', and used the ideas of thinkers such as Hayek and Nozick to pursue their aims, but they were not anarchists. They sought to reduce the impact of the state, but not to destroy it. Indeed, as Jenkins (1995) pointed out, Thatcher was certainly not averse to using the power of the state to achieve her supposedly anti-statist aims.

However, we can state that all politicians, whether fame is the spur or not, start with some set of convictions, which mean they join one party rather than another, or become motivated by one issue rather than something else. There are certain beliefs and arguments from which they will not resile (King, 1996). Mrs Thatcher's ideas and attitudes were formed well before she became the leader of her party, an event, in any case, that was deemed highly unlikely until it actually occurred in 1975 (Berlinski, 2008). Certainly, Mrs Thatcher was ambitious and driven, and she made compromises along the way, but we can state with some certainty that there were some views that she would simply not accept. The same can be said for Gordon Brown and most other politicians who have taken many years to get from their initial interest in politics to positions of power. No matter how ambitious a politician might be, there can be no certainty that they will ever reach a position of influence – after all, most aspiring politicians fail to reach high office. Moreover, if personal ambition were the only consideration why would anyone have become active in the Labour Party in the early 1980s (like Brown and Blair), or the Conservative Party in the late 1990s (like Cameron and Osborne); why would anyone join a minority party? We must presume that people do these apparently irrational acts because of what they believe in.

We might argue, in answer to these comments on intentions, that what matter are not aims but the effects that a policy has had. This is indeed important: a policy must ultimately be judged by what it does, not what it meant to do or why it was introduced. Jones and Murie (2006, p 33) are critical of the Conservatives for seeing the RTB 'as an end in itself'. The RTB, they say,

> was a mechanism for increasing owner occupation and for responding to the desire of some tenants to own their properties. It was not a means of achieving any other housing objective and the response to questions from the Environment Committee during its inquiry into the sale of council houses in 1979 and 1980 was largely to brush aside other issues. The issues about the loss of relets, the financial implications of the policy, or whether or not the policy would contribute to the development of welfare housing, were almost dismissed. These concerns, from the Government's perspective, missed the point and the simpler intent of policy. (p 33)

Jones and Murie are critical of the Conservatives for single-mindedly pursuing a policy on the basis of those who benefited from and supported it and not the wider effects of the policy. However, they do not seek to suggest why such a 'simpler intent' was not valid and worthwhile in itself. The criticism appears to be that the Conservatives were concentrating on the 'wrong things', even though they were only doing what they promised to do if elected. Instead, Jones and

Murie seem to be saying that the Conservatives should have concentrated on priorities set by others.

However, a concern for wider effects and impacts is hardly a neutral concern in itself. Any evidence of these effects will need to be interpreted to determine its significance, and this act of interpretation will inevitably be based on our presuppositions and prejudices. The critics of the RTB do not suspend their formative beliefs when analysing the data on the RTB. Instead these beliefs form the prism through which the data are represented. We take particular things as significant because of our starting position. We choose to discard certain facts in favour of others and so find we are capable of making the evidence suit our desired conclusions.

So a concern for 'effects' might merely be part of an attempt to prejudge the RTB, by refusing to come to terms with what it was intended to do; or, rather, by presuming that the RTB was introduced for the reasons the critic deems significant. Instead, we need to view the RTB not just on its impact and outputs, but on how they relate to what might be seen as the inputs to the policy. By this I mean the RTB's aims and intentions, the reasoning behind the policy and its particular formulation. Therefore the next part of this chapter is concerned with looking at some of the justification and reasoning for the RTB. My main source is material published by the Conservative Party leading up to the 1979 election, including the election manifesto of that year.

What Mrs Thatcher meant to do

The RTB was developed in the context of political and economic upheaval. Edward Heath's Conservative government had sought to deal with a housing bubble (perhaps of its own creation), an oil crisis and a series of industrial disputes. Heath went to the country in February 1974 with a slogan of 'Who rules Britain?' and the electorate decided they did not wish him to, but favoured a minority Labour administration (Ramsden, 1998). Later in 1974, the Prime Minister, Harold Wilson, went to the country again and was returned with a small majority, which was itself eroded over time. The election of a Labour government did little to deal with the economic and political problems facing the country. The culmination of this crisis came when the government sought an emergency loan to keep the public services running from the International Monetary Fund, a body ostensibly existing to support developing countries. The Conservative opposition, particularly under its new leader, Margaret Thatcher, was therefore able to present a case for a change of direction in the context of a government which was seen to have lost control of events.

The change in direction of the Conservatives also took place in the context of an intellectual shift which saw a resurgence in right-wing and liberal ideas (Green, 1987). Along with the feeling that the post-war political and economic consensus had failed was a sense that the received ideas on the role of the state and markets were no longer sufficient to deal with the problems facing developed countries.

The development of the so-called 'New Right' provided much of the intellectual support for the Conservatives in the UK and the Republicans in the US (Green, 1987). There was a greater receptivity towards right-of-centre ideas shown in the award of the Nobel Prize for economics to Friedrich Hayek in 1974 and Milton Friedman in 1976. The 1970s also saw the rise of several influential think tanks, such as the Institute of Economic Affairs (which had existed to promote free-market ideas since the 1950s), the Adam Smith Institute and the Centre for Policy Studies (set up by the Conservative politician, Sir Keith Joseph, as a base for what would become known as Thatcherism).

In hindsight, of course, we can see the changes since 1979 as inevitable and almost natural. After more than 30 years, which have seen a considerable transformation in politics and the reorientation of the main political parties, it is easy to see the changes proposed by the Conservatives as being more prescriptive and certain than they actually were at the time. We therefore forget how much of what the Conservatives were proposing was a radical break with the post-war consensus. Yet what becomes very clear in reading Conservative documents from the late 1970s is the sheer intellectual confidence with which they were stated. These documents were not in any way tentative or hedged with emollient language. There was no search for a consensus here, but rather the belief that the Labour government was taking the country in the wrong direction and that the Conservative position was that of the majority. Unlike more recent documents and debates, this material is full of ideas and arguments rather than a concern for presentation and sound bites. It is clear that there was a particular ideological position that underpinned these arguments and there was no particular attempt to hide it.

Of course, this is the talk of a party in opposition, and so one that was not actually doing anything other than talk. Yet, unlike the situation after 1983, this was not a period of landslides and 100-seat majorities. The three elections since 1970 had been reasonably close and so the opposition party could realistically plan for office.

In 1976 the Conservatives published a document entitled *The Right Approach* (Conservative Party, 1976). This was a major document (over 23,000 words) outlining what might be termed the Thatcherite position. Accordingly, it is worthwhile looking at this document in some depth to establish the main elements of this position, and how a general philosophical position is linked by the Conservatives to owner occupation and the sale of council houses.

What is noticeable is the stridency of the language, giving a sense of Britain facing an imminent emergency, and the notion that socialism is a real threat:

> It is the task of the Conservative Party today to restore hope and confidence to a disillusioned British people. Without the prospect of an alternative government with realistic policies, offending neither against common sense nor against the instincts of the majority, the very survival of parliamentary democracy could be threatened – by the

increasing alienation of the electors, if not in the end by direct action
from exasperated pressure groups. (Conservative Party, 1976, p 7)

More than 30 years on we might see this as an example of excessive hyperbole,
but it shows that the Conservatives at this point were not seeking consensus.
The country was going in a dangerous direction which was out of step with the
majority. What it also shows is that this document was not just a statement of
policy, but had a more ambitious aim to expound a critique of socialism and to
provide a coherent and grounded alternative.

Of course, the Conservative Party had always opposed socialism and in this
regard we might see policies such as the RTB as consistent with long-standing
Conservative principles. Indeed, Green (2006, p 42) suggests that promoting
owner occupation through policies like the RTB was consistent with 'the late
nineteenth- and early twentieth-century Conservative idea of spreading property
ownership to strengthen the "ramparts of property" against Socialist assault'. It
was, Green argues, 'in keeping with long-established Conservative goals' (2006,
p 42). This is certainly the case, but we might also argue that Mrs Thatcher and
her supporters also felt that this link with a Conservative past had been diluted
or even lost by the actions of successive post-war Conservative governments
that had compromised with social democracy. What they sought, therefore, was
a return to an older and purer form of Conservatism.

A key fault of socialism is the problem of heightened 'class feeling' (Conservative
Party, 1976, p 14), which is manifested in terms of the Labour government's links
with the trades unions and, importantly, council housing:

> The antagonisms and bitterness that exist in our society now have little
> or nothing to do with 'class' in the traditional sense. They are for the
> most part the results of Socialism in action: for example, the political
> fomentation of industrial unrest, the relative strength of unionised and
> non-unionised labour, and the feudal system of municipal housing.
> (Conservative Party, 1976, p 15)[2]

The manner in which the Labour Party governs creates 'class feeling' through the
social divisions resulting from their industrial and housing policies.

The Conservatives wish to counter this policy of division through what they
call 'a philosophy of balance', which is based on 'rights and duties' (Conservative
Party, 1976, p 16). It is worth quoting from the document here at some length
to get some sense of what this philosophy entails:

> For answers which are relevant to Britain's real problems, and which
> are based on a philosophical approach that matches 'the manners, the
> customs, the laws, the traditions' of the British people, the country
> will need to turn to the Conservative Party.

> Man is both an individual and a social being, and all political philosophies have sought to accommodate these two, often conflicting, elements in human nature. Conservatism has always represented a balance between the two, arguing against Liberal individualists for man's social role and against Socialists for the right of the individual to develop as far and as fast as he can, choosing freely from a wide range of opportunities while recognising his duties towards his fellows.
>
> We have laid particular stress on the individual and his freedom in recent years because Socialism has tipped the balance so far the other way. Moreover, many of the developments of modern industrial society have tended to dehumanise life and threaten the individuality and independence of men and women. (Conservative Party, 1976, pp 16–17)

The Conservatives see themselves as working with the traditions of the country which involve a balance between the rights of the individual and their duties to others. They portray themselves as standing between atomism and corporatism. The Conservatives argue that stressing individual rights has become necessary because of the excesses of socialism which they see has undermined individual rights.

Having defined this philosophy of balance they link this to property:

> What we have to set out, and it is in the main stream of Conservatism for us to do so, is a political philosophy that goes beyond the State and the individual, and begins to express in human terms the complex network of reciprocal rights and duties in an orderly society.
>
> Such a philosophy will recognise that private ownership of property is essential if we are to encourage personal responsibility and the freedom that goes with it. Property diffuses power, increases choice and is an important source of independence. Since some people have more ability and a greater opportunity to acquire property than others, there are bound to be social and economic inequalities. Conservatives are not egalitarians. We believe in levelling up, in enhancing opportunities, not in levelling down, which dries up the springs of enterprise and endeavour and ultimately means that there are fewer resources for helping the disadvantaged. Hostility to success, because success brings inequality, is often indistinguishable from envy and greed, especially when, as Alexander Solzhenitsyn has pointed out, it is dressed up in the language of the 'class struggle'. (Conservative Party, 1976, pp 17–18)

We get a sense here of the intellectual confidence of the Conservatives, where they are prepared to offer clear and sophisticated justification for their arguments rather than relying on sound bites and presentation. They see property rights as a means of raising people up and encouraging enterprise. The consequence of this is a degree of inequality, but this, the Conservatives argue, is necessary to ensure that power is diffused through society and individuals are able to express choice.

They wish to go beyond simplistic class divisions – of us and them – to stress the full complexity of human society. Society is based on reciprocity, of mutual respect, restraint and order, in which individuals respect the needs of others. This, they suggest, is a basic notion that underpins ordinary life:

> The balance which we seek has its roots not only in a distinctive, if too rarely articulated, Conservative approach, but also in basic common sense. That has always been one of the great strengths of Conservatism. The facts of life invariably *do* turn out to be Tory. (Conservative Party, 1976, p 19, original emphasis)

As we saw in Chapter 2, conservatism is dispositional and often goes unspoken. Scruton (2001) pointed to the inarticulate nature of conservatism that is based on how people actually think, feel and act. The Conservative document echoes this, making a link to basic common sense. The last sentence of this quote, which is tantamount to saying that 'reality is Conservatism', is perhaps the most obvious example of the renewed confidence of the Conservatives. It is a wonderfully provocative statement, and one that shows that the Conservatives had left behind them any notion of consensus. Rather this was a committed party that had a clear sense of purpose. Also we might state that it was by no means an inarticulate one.

Towards the end of the document, after considering a full range of policies, the Conservatives are able to show how their philosophy of balance underpins their programme for government:

> Our policies are designed to restore and defend individual freedom and responsibility. We mean to protect the individual from excessive interference by the State or by organisations licensed by the State, to stop the drift of power away from the people and their democratic institutions, and to give them more power as citizens, as owners and as consumers. We shall do this by better financial management, by reducing the proportion of the nation's wealth consumed by the State, by steadily easing the burden of Britain's debts, by lowering taxes when we can, by encouraging home ownership, by taking the first steps towards making this country a nation of worker owners, by giving parents a greater say in the better education of their children. (Conservative Party, 1976, p 71)

As I have stated, the document covers the full range of policy. As seen in the reference to property, they seek to justify a larger role for owner occupation. They wish to encourage the tenure for three reasons:

>First, it gives people independence; the ownership of their home buttresses a family's freedom. Second, largely for this reason, most people want to become home-owners, and are happier as home-owners than as tenants. Third, helping people to become home-owners represents an excellent bargain for the taxpayer; the average subsidies on a newly built council house add up to about £1,300 in the first year, while tax relief on an average new mortgage is around £300. (Conservative Party, 1976, p 51)

Owner occupation is justified, therefore, because it enhances freedom, it makes people happier and so they wish more of it, and because it is cheaper for the tax-payer relative to social housing. The first reason is consonant with the Conservatives' position on the importance of property and how this allows for rights and duties to be expressed within society. The second reason shows that the Conservatives have not completely relegated electoral concerns. They recognise that owner occupation is popular and so they support it accordingly. Their third point is an important link to policy in that the Conservatives argue that owner occupation represents better value for money than social renting. They suggest that promoting owning at the expense of council housing will save the tax-payer a considerable amount of money.

What these three reasons for supporting owner occupation show is a mix of principle and pragmatism. The Conservatives – who, as we have seen, argue that they are merely stating the 'facts of life' – see that their principles are linked to reality in a very direct sense. They are thus able to see a happy connection between their philosophy of common sense and pleasing the tax-payer.

The third reason presents a justification for the RTB. They see owner occupation as cheaper and better value for money. But they extend this argument considerably and outline some of the practical elements of a policy of selling council houses:

>We wish, once and for all, to get rid of the unfair restrictions on the sale of their homes to council tenants and new town tenants. We believe they should have the statutory right to buy their homes after three years occupancy either on a freehold basis or, in the case of flats in England and Wales, on a leasehold basis. A practical method would be to allow tenants to serve notice on the council, with access to the courts if the council refused the tenant's request to purchase or if it was obstructive.
>
>We envisage council home sales being financed by building society and insurance company mortgages as well as local authority mortgages. The small cost of tax relief on additional mortgages would be more than offset by the increased revenue that would flow from a large programme of council home sales.
>
>Local authorities are expensive and not always efficient providers of homes. It is doubtful whether many urban authorities add to the

housing stock at all. Much local authority new building is essentially an expensive process of bull-dozing neighbourhoods into piles of rubble, with a switch within the rented sector from private to public.

The housing stock now exceeds the number of households by over three-quarters of a million homes, and demand for council housing has been artificially inflated by ever more heavily subsidised rents (which 'oblige' councils to build, since relatively few re-lets are available), and by legislation which has ensured a sharply diminishing stock of private accommodation for rent. (Conservative Party, 1976, pp 52–3)

This quote contains key elements of the eventual policy, but interestingly makes no specific mention of discounts to encourage sales. Instead the document emphasises the use of capital receipts as a means of offsetting increased costs (these were costs to the Treasury and so the implication is that this increased revenue would not be at the disposal of local councils). The tone of this passage is negative and concentrates on a critique of council housing and how it is funded. The implication of this argument is that tenants are being unreasonably held back from purchasing by their landlords. Indeed, a voluntary system of council house sales had been introduced by the Heath government (Sillars, 2007), but this policy was no longer encouraged by the Labour government elected in 1974. Giving this policy a statutory basis would allow tenants to express their desires. Implicitly it would also inhibit what the Conservatives saw as the wasteful and destructive habits of councils as landlords and house builders.

By 1978 this proposal for a statutory right had been firmed up to include financial incentives. In a confidential paper presented by Michael Heseltine to the Shadow Cabinet dated 28 June 1978, a definitive proposal is presented for achieving an increase in house sales and the expansion of owner occupation (Heseltine, 1978). Heseltine outlines three arguments to justify the RTB. First is what he terms the 'political and social argument' (p 1) of spreading wealth and ownership and therefore independence from the state. Second, Heseltine presents the 'economic argument' (p 1), outlining the higher levels of subsidy for council housing and the fact that tenants often pay more in rent than the value of the dwelling. He sees selling council houses as financially beneficial for both the individual household and the state. Third, Heseltine considers the 'democratic argument' (p 1) where 'by increasing the availability of home ownership we are meeting an overwhelming public demand' (p 2). Selling council houses is deemed to be what people want, as is extending owner occupation generally.

In terms of promoting the sale of council houses, Heseltine proposes discounts of 30% to 50% based on length of tenancy. Interestingly, however, he juxtaposes this with an alternative proposal of increasing rents considerably. However, he recognises with some understatement that any 'sudden increase would cause much political difficulty' (p 2). Instead, he clearly prefers a positive policy that offers incentives rather than a punitive approach. Accordingly, he not only proposes offering discounts but also the right to 100% mortgages and what he terms 'realistic valuations' (p 2) based on the fact that the dwelling is on a council estate.

Heseltine also discusses the use of capital receipts and makes it clear that the first call on this should be to clear outstanding loan debts on the property. However, he then states that what is left over should be shared between the Treasury and the council 'in some proportions as to leave the council with a substantial incentive to sell' (p 3). This last point is interesting because, of course, we might have thought that giving tenants a statutory right makes any incentives to landlords somewhat irrelevant.

A more radical suggestion had been provided by Peter Walker, who when Environment Secretary in the Heath government had introduced the earlier voluntary system (Sillars, 2007). His suggestion was actually to give the dwellings away to long-term tenants. Walker felt this would be most expedient and certainly popular and could be justified on the basis of past rent payments. However, Green (2006) states that Mrs Thatcher resisted this proposal on the grounds of how this would appear to what she called 'our people', those according to Green, 'who had struggled to pay mortgages on their homes' (p 20). What this shows is that the sense of personal responsibility also limited the role and extent of the policy. Giving council dwellings away would be seen as unreasonable to those who had saved and paid their way. If the Conservatives wanted to see the extension of middle-class values then disbursing free gifts was not a means of achieving it.

So the policy was largely formed nearly a year before the 1979 election and was based on a clear justification consistent with what might be seen as a coherent philosophy for government. The Conservative election manifesto therefore rehearsed what were by now a set of familiar arguments.

As part of the opening statement in the manifesto the Conservatives state:

> We want to work *with the grain* of human nature, helping people to help themselves – and others. This is the way to restore that self-reliance and self-confidence which are the basis of personal responsibility and national success. (Conservative Party, 1979, Section 1, original emphasis)

There is no mention of a specific philosophy here, but we can see this as a simplified statement of a core belief, emphasising responsibility and self-reliance. Likewise, their criticism of the Labour government's housing policy is more muted, if no less clear: 'Unlike Labour, we want more people to have the security and satisfaction of owning property' (Section 3).

The manifesto clearly and succinctly outlines a policy on council house sales that follows the Heseltine proposals:

> Many families who live on council estates and in new towns would like to buy their own homes but either cannot afford to or are prevented by the local authority or the Labour government. The time has come

to end these restrictions. In the first session of the next Parliament we shall therefore give council and new town tenants the legal right to buy their homes, while recognising the special circumstances of rural areas and sheltered housing for the elderly. Subject to safeguards over resale, the terms we propose would allow a discount on market values reflecting the fact that council tenants effectively have security of tenure. Our discounts will range from 33 per cent after three years, rising with length of tenancy to a maximum of 50 per cent after twenty years. We shall also ensure that 100 per cent mortgages are available for the purchase of council and new town houses. We shall introduce a right for these tenants to obtain limited term options on their homes so that they know in advance the price at which they can buy, while they save the money to do so. (Conservative Party, 1979, Section 5)

This policy is presented as a priority, in that they commit themselves to introducing legislation at the earliest opportunity after the election. It is clear that this policy has been thought over and honed. Potential objections, such as the supply of rural dwellings and sheltered housing, have been dealt with, as have the practicalities of valuations and household decision making. Households are to be given some certainty with the valuation fixed for a set period of time.

What we can learn from this discussion is that the RTB was developed over time and was informed out of principle. It was not an opportunistic or populist gesture, but a policy that was based on clear thinking, a coherent approach to the role of the state and individuals within society and a critique of existing provision. The Conservatives, we can state therefore, knew what they were doing. The RTB became such an iconic policy because of how it connected with a particular philosophy of government, and so could be readily articulated, justified and understood.

There was something simple and enticing about the policy, as we can see by the very concise manner in which the Conservatives were able to state the policy in their 1979 election manifesto. The policy did not require any special jargon to justify it or any complex set of arguments, as was the case with many housing policies before or since. The RTB could be explained using simple language and with concepts all could understand. The mechanisms underpinning it were clear – one applied, received a valuation which stood for a set period of time and had the right to a mortgage – and so were the incentives in the form of an upfront discount. Once established, then, we can see why the policy did not take much selling.

What Mrs Thatcher did

As I have stated earlier, the RTB did not exactly emerge out of nothing. Previous Conservative governments had sought to promote the sale of council houses, but had not given tenants a statutory right (Sillars, 2007). The result was a patchy pattern of sales, which depended on the particular local authority (Jones and Murie, 2006). The Conservatives by the mid-1970s saw this position as unsatisfactory. They saw a pent-up desire to own on the part of many council tenants and so were determined to act decisively. So what did the policy of the RTB actually involve?

The measures were included in the 1980 Housing Act in England and Wales and the 1980 Housing Tenants Rights Etc. (Scotland) Act was largely consistent with the proposals considered earlier. The discretion that local authorities had as to whether to sell their dwelling was replaced by a statutory right for secure tenants of at least three years standing to buy their dwelling. This applied to most secure tenants, including tenants of councils, new towns and non-charitable housing associations. Some types of dwelling, such as sheltered units for the elderly and those in rural areas, were excluded. However, in general, the aim was to include as many dwellings as possible. Guidance was produced to ensure a degree of commonality in procedures and administration across the country and the Secretary of State gained powers to intervene and monitor the process. The belief, which turned out to be substantiated (Malpass and Murie, 1999), was that some councils would seek to obstruct tenants from exercising their rights.

The legislation outlined a method of valuing properties and a system of discounts based on length of tenancy (which need not only relate to the current dwelling). Tenants could qualify for the RTB after three years with a 33% discount. This would increase at 1% per annum up to a maximum of 50%. If the tenants sold the property within one to five years they would have to repay all or part of the discount, with the repayment reducing by 20% for every complete year.

Another aspect consistent with the manifesto was the right to a 100% mortgage with conditions set by the Secretary of State. Valuations could also be frozen for up to two years should a tenant wish to defer purchase.

All these measures suggest a well worked out policy that had considered some of the key problems of implementation such as resistance from local authorities and the problems of the supply of certain types of specialist accommodation. However, the RTB has been amended and changed many times during its life. Under the Conservatives, these changes have largely been to extend the system, whilst changes since 1997 have been more restrictive.

In 1984 the qualification period was reduced to two years and the maximum discount increased to 60%. Two years later, the 1986 Housing and Planning Act increased discounts for flats to a starting point of 44% increasing by 2% increments to a maximum of 70%. The government was concerned that sales of flats had been slower than those of houses and so sought to encourage this.

One restriction under the Conservatives came with the 1988 Housing Act, which removed the RTB for all new housing association tenants, who became assured rather than secure tenants. The reason for this was largely to ensure that the main elements in the 1988 Act, particularly the use of private finance, would be viable. It was felt that private financiers would be reluctant to lend money for housing association development if tenants could buy these assets after a short period.

The Labour government elected in 1997 was committed to maintaining the RTB, but it did seek to restrict the level of discounts. In 1999 maximum discounts were limited across England and Wales to a range between £22,000 (for low-cost areas) to £38,000 (in London). In 2003 this was changed again so that in all but the most expensive areas of the South East and London (which remained at £38,000), discounts were reduced to a maximum of £16,000. Similar restrictions also apply in Wales.

Further restrictions were introduced in the 2004 Housing Act, which increased the qualifying period from two to five years. Another important change was that those who wished to sell their dwelling within 10 years were obliged to offer it at market value to their former landlord or their successor organisation (this caveat was necessary due to stock transfer). In June 2009, the government announced it would consult on whether local authorities should keep all the capital receipts from their RTB sales.

A similar pattern of restrictions was introduced in Scotland. A so-called 'modernised' RTB was introduced in 2001 which sought to set the rights of tenants alongside the needs of the community. Accordingly, the qualification period was extended from two to five years, discounts were restricted to a maximum of £15,000 and the distinction between houses and flats was abolished. But the most significant change was a procedure to designate certain areas as 'pressurised', where the RTB could be suspended. The Scottish government could now suspend the RTB for up to five years in these designated pressurised areas on the basis of a request from the local authority. Local authorities could argue that housing need in their area was so pressing that the RTB should not apply. Perhaps inevitably this is a designation that several councils have sought to exploit.

As well as restricting the RTB, all these changes over the years have created a much more complex situation. Instead of the simplicity and understandability of the original 1980 system there are now many caveats and restrictions to the system. Clearly the aim of these changes has been to limit the impact of the RTB. However, the problem from the point of view of social housing, as we shall see in the next chapter, is that the majority of sales took place in the 1980s before these restrictions were imposed. Critics of the RTB might argue that these restrictions were necessary precisely because of the effects of the policy in its first 10 years. But we might also suggest that as most of the tenants who desired to purchase had done so, the political and electoral costs of restricting the RTB were considerably minimised. By the late 1990s it was politically safe to limit discounts and extend qualifying periods because most tenants were either not eligible, due to stock transfer to housing associations (where no new tenants had the RTB), or were not in stable employment and dependent on Housing Benefit and so could not afford to buy.

These are issues that we shall consider in more detail in subsequent chapters, but what is important to bear in mind is that supposedly left-of-centre governments in England and Scotland have not felt able to repeal the RTB. It maintains its status as a key housing policy, even as its significance has declined since the 1980s. The policy caught the imagination of many people, be they tenants or political commentators, and it became one of the iconic policies of the Thatcher period. Its success is such that it can be modified but not abolished. It is too firmly a part of the housing systems of the UK. This was seen in early 2009 when the housing press began to report the effect of declining RTB sales due to the credit crunch.[3] Instead of seeing this as a cause of celebration, many within local authorities saw it as a serious problem because it was dramatically reducing their available capital receipts and so harming their ability to meet their statutory commitments. Many local authorities have become dependent on the RTB and so we can suggest that it had become a normal, taken-for-granted part of the housing system. Local authorities are operating in a milieu shaped by the RTB and they are still dependent on it. In the following chapter we shall consider this issue of the decline of the RTB as a prelude to a full discussion on the impact of the policy. However, the main point of this chapter has been to show that the RTB had roots; that it did not come out of the ether, but was grounded in a coherent set of beliefs which seemed to resonate with a genuine desire to own. The result is that tenants, landlords, policy makers and commentators operate in a housing world formed by the RTB.

Notes
[1] A particular example from the right is Anne Coulter (1998; 2005).

[2] Interestingly in these documents a capital 'S' is always used for 'Socialism', as if to emphasise the dangerous nature of the concept.

[3] We shall discuss this development more fully in Chapter 4.

FOUR

What happened next?

Introduction

As we saw at the end of Chapter 3, one of the somewhat perverse consequences of the credit crunch in 2008 has been the reaction of local authorities to a sharp decline in Right to Buy (RTB) sales. Perhaps inevitably sales have declined quite considerably as a result of the collapse in the housing market generally. In England RTB sales in the third quarter of 2008 compared with the same period in 2007 have reportedly fallen by an average of 85% and in Wales by 82% (*Inside Housing*, 20 February 2009). In some local authorities there had been no sales in the period, and all parts of the country appeared to be equally affected.

However, instead of seeing the fall-off in sales as a cause for celebration, in that more housing is potentially available in the future, the response has been one of crisis and panic. Local authorities are only able to use 25% of RTB receipts, but the fall in receipts is still making a considerable dent in the capital programmes of many local authorities. This means that councils will have to restrict their spending on improvements and renovations. *Inside Housing*, 20 February 2009, reports that spending per dwelling in one area – Wolverhampton – will reduce from a planned £680 to £310 per annum by 2011. The problem is that many local authorities have factored a steady and predictable stream of RTB sales into their business plans.

This response to the decline in the RTB is, I would argue, particularly instructive. Instead of the RTB being seen as problematic, as is the case with much academic discussion, many local authorities see it as necessary. The RTB is here viewed as a permanent and expected part of the housing system on which local authorities are now dependent. A regular and predictable flow of RTB sales has formed part of their financial calculations and so it helps to make the financial system operate. Both the government and councils can be said to rely on this income and problems arise when the RTB falls off.

So instead of this recession being seen as an ideal opportunity to end the RTB as some critics are suggesting (as we discuss in the next chapter), the possible end of the RTB (by accident if not design) is actually taken as a serious dilemma which compromises the ability of local authorities to meet their commitments. The crisis over the collapse in sales shows how the RTB has become a necessary part of UK housing. It is now so well established that certain agencies depend on it and would suffer were it no longer to be there. The RTB could not easily be repealed without considerable expense and upheaval, despite the critics who see it as an unreasonable and expensive subsidy which only a fortunate minority benefit from. The RTB is in fact interlinked with other policies affecting finance, maintenance and refurbishment. This, in turn, suggests that there may well be enough vested interests *within* the local authority sector to protect it from abolition, unless, of course, the government is able to provide an alternative source of finance. We might also suggest that the benefits of the RTB actually do go beyond the ex-tenants who have used it. Current tenants benefit in that a stream of capital receipts has been used to improve their dwellings.

More generally this seeming paradox – of councils bemoaning the decline in the loss of their dwellings, while relying upon the created stream of capital receipts – demonstrates that we now operate within what might be called a *post-RTB* world. By that I mean we are now in a situation where the RTB, established for 30 years, is such a normal part of the environment that its loss would be seriously destabilising. What this shows is the importance of pragmatism, which will often override principle, especially where money is involved and where there is no alternative. Secure tenants have had statutory rights since 1980 and local authorities cannot avoid the consequences. They have therefore shifted their thinking and their operations in such a way as to maximise the benefits that can accrue from structures which they are unable to affect.

In this chapter we shall consider the wider effects of the RTB, including, among other things, what effect the RTB had on other tenures and whether it can be seen as the cause or major contributor to the residualisation of social housing. I want to consider what has happened with the RTB over its 30 years, and to look at how we should view it in terms of other policies, but also why it has declined. This will involve looking at some of the key data to form a sense of the RTB's impact. We shall then consider this impact more fully, plunging into some of the controversies surrounding the policy and its effects. Of course, the reason that the RTB is controversial is because it can be viewed in different ways and I want to explore this, again to ensure a fresh and different approach to the RTB. Only certain arguments are ever rehearsed in the literature and we need to be aware that there are a variety of possible approaches that we can take to the RTB and that our choice of approach will affect how we see the various effects of the RTB, and indeed which ones we view seriously and which we downplay.

A key insight that comes out of this discussion is what might be called the competitive nature of the RTB and its effects. The debate tends to stress the benefits or problems for one group or another, whilst ignoring the effects on others. Those on the right tend to concentrate on the liberation of households from social housing and the creation of new owners and do not tend to dwell much on homelessness or problems with supply. This is because they see greater benefits to owner occupation and consider social housing to be a problem. The supporters of social housing will stress the decline in re-lets, the increase in homelessness and reduction in choice, but, in doing so, ignore or reject any benefits of owning. We need to remember that all policies involve a degree of competition or necessitate some trade-off: if I succeed in renting a private sector flat, others will miss out; if I am allocated a council house, others cannot have it;

if my offer to buy the house is accepted by the sellers, others are rejected. Most situations in housing are to this extent competitive and will remain so as long as there are imbalances in supply and demand.

Yet, as the discussion on the financial consequences of the decline in sales shows, it is not really just a case of balancing one side against the other. Those bodies who we would have thought would have welcomed the decline actually see it as a crucial loss of capital finance which will hamper them. Housing systems evolve and players within the system adapt to new conditions once they see the advantages or necessity of doing so. If the government imposes a policy onto local authorities they have to adapt and change as best they can, and this they have done. Thus, whilst some might retain the competitive sense of policies – the RTB against the integrity of social housing, for instance – for others the issue is how best to survive and thrive in a particular milieu that will not disappear just because they can see it has a certain number of faults.

The focus of this book up to this point has been deliberately narrow. This has allowed us to focus on the RTB and how it was justified. We have taken seriously the narrow and simple purpose of the Conservatives and seen what the RTB was meant to do. However, we now need to broaden the discussion out somewhat to consider what actually happened once the RTB was implemented and was taken up in such large numbers. We need to consider the effect on social housing and those who remained tenants. But the approach we have taken in this book, from narrow to broad, will allow us to retain a sense of what the RTB was meant to do. The purpose of the RTB was not to help social housing and we need to remember this: judging the RTB in terms of its effects on social housing might be important to some commentators, but it is not sufficient.

In any debate on the RTB what matters is where we start from. So, for example, do we begin with the idea of individual freedom and personal choice and so see increasing owner occupation as particularly important? Alternatively, do we wish to deal with urgent housing need and to assist the vulnerable to find secure and affordable housing? Do we place greater importance on personal responsibility or social solidarity? Depending on what starting point we have, the RTB can be seen as either transformative or a disaster.

However, the actual situation is rather more nuanced than this. Whilst we might wish to see the RTB in terms of a left versus right split, there are some on the left who have always supported the sale of council houses. One example of this is Frank Field, who began arguing for such a policy in the mid-1970s (Field, 1976; Ward, 1985). However, there are those on the libertarian right who support the extension of owner occupation, but do not agree that this should be subsidised in any way. They see it as entirely legitimate and desirable to sell council houses, but only at open market values. A different argument, with the same effect, is to question whether it is ever justified to subsidise owner occupation, particularly as households will then have an appreciating asset which they will be able to sell at a profit or pass on to their children.

Carrying on in the same vein, there are those who argue against social engineering of any kind, seeing it as illegitimate for government to seek to determine a particular set of outcomes. In response to this, others, still on the right of the spectrum, might argue that owner occupation should be supported as a means of creating and maintaining social stability, and the RTB more specifically as a means of dealing with economic dependency and state control. In this sense, it might be argued that the ends justify the means, and that the social transformation caused by greater levels of owner occupation justifies state intervention. So there are plenty of arguments within the political right over the efficacy and ethics of the RTB.[1]

Within social housing we can see a range of views, with many who work in the sector opposed to the RTB because it reduces their ability to help the most vulnerable and because it has meant the loss of the best dwellings. Yet, as we have seen, there are also some within the sector who see the RTB's decline as a financial problem and so would seek numbers to increase. It might also be the case that many who oppose the RTB have been persuaded that it was simply too popular to be repealed, including John Prescott, who had responsibility for housing in the Blair government for much of the period between 1997 and 2007. Elected governments have to remain aware of what is popular even if this might mean treating some people better than others, or favouring current households over future ones.

So in considering the impact of a particular policy we need to be aware that there is no one particular position from which to start, and that any evaluation depends on where the critic starts from and what he or she considers to be important. We have sought to deal with this, as far as we can, by initially taking the RTB on its own terms. So in any evaluation we need to remain aware that the RTB is bound up by a series of diverse interests and this might mean that certain people reach somewhat surprising conclusions.

What did happen?

The first priority for us is to comprehend the scale of the policy. As we have seen in Chapter 3, the Conservatives were confident that they were working with the grain of human nature. The RTB, they felt, was what many council tenants wanted. Of course, most politicians show certainty and confidence when they announce proposals. In this case, however, they appear to have been right. Table 4.1 shows the scale of RTB sales in each part of Great Britain.

The first and most important point to make is that the RTB created just over 2.5 million new owner-occupiers. It is quite easy to be blasé about this, but this is actually quite a huge number. Indeed, when we consider that there were only 2.6 million council dwellings in Britain in 2006 (Wilcox, 2008) we can see just what impact it did have. As we discussed in Chapter 3, the Conservatives in 1979–80 took a deliberately narrow view of the policy: it was about allowing tenants to become owner-occupiers and breaking the influence that councils had

Table 4.1: RTB sales

Year	England	Scotland	Wales	Great Britain
1980	55	2,157	0	2,212
1981	66,321	10,096	7,196	84,333
1982	174,697	13,544	16,088	204,329
1983	120,659	17,321	9,088	147,208
1984	86,315	15,248	5,650	107,213
1985	78,433	14,473	5,622	98,328
1986	77,144	13,322	5,420	95,856
1987	86,845	18,594	5,609	111,048
1988	132,980	31,480	9,605	174,065
1989	144,754	38,443	12,753	195,950
1990	96,729	32,535	6,487	135,751
1991	53,462	22,694	3,503	79,659
1992	42,280	23,521	3,823	68,624
1993	42,034	19,787	2,814	63,635
1994	45,875	21,128	3,132	70,135
1995	34,553	16,636	2,369	53,558
1996	34,161	13,023	2,093	49,277
1997	44,375	17,369	2,632	64,376
1998	44,256	14,948	2,614	61,818
1999	58,462	14,227	3,466	76,155
2000	61,956	14,935	3,522	80,413
2001	58,955	14,095	3,446	76,496
2002	68996	17,343	4,288	90,627
2003	85,934	20,698	6,924	113,556
2004	67,160	15,203	5,063	87,426
2005	36,353	13,033	2,090	51,376
2006	24,190	10,487	1,366	36,043
2007	16,410	7,420	1,017	24,847
Total	**1,884,214**	**483,560**	**137,540**	**2,505,314**

Source: Wilcox (1999; 2008).

over housing. If we take this narrow concern then we have to see the RTB as a great success. Nearly 40% of council housing has been converted into owner-occupied housing and 2.5 million households gained access to an asset and the financial independence and personal responsibility that the Conservatives saw as important to creating a post-socialist society.

Indeed, it is hard to conceive of another housing policy that comes close to having this effect in terms of sheer scale. The only contender is the obvious one of council housing itself, with over 6 million dwellings being built, largely between 1923 and 1980. But even here the timescale is considerably longer. Most other housing policies are of much less impact and on a smaller scale, despite the rhetoric that may support them. Both the Blair and Brown governments have introduced grandiosely titled policies such as the Sustainable Communities Plan (ODPM, 2003) and Homes for All (ODPM, 2005), as well as plans to rescue the mortgage market, yet the scale of these has been tiny in comparison to the sweep of the RTB.

Of course, the RTB had a built-in advantage in comparison to any other policy, including the building of council housing. This was the simple fact that the resources for the policy were readily available. The direct cost of the RTB, compared with mass house building, was negligible and much of this did not fall directly on central government but was rather borne by local authorities as the owners of the stock. The RTB could have an immediate impact because there were 6 million possible properties to be sold. It did not need a lengthy or expensive lead-in to create the resources for the policy. The RTB also did not involve a tremendous upheaval on the part of the households concerned; they could become owner-occupiers without even moving. So there was a simplicity to the RTB. We can see it as a once-in-a-generation policy, which benefited from a happy confluence of supply, demand, opportunity and system design, and this is shown readily in the figures.

Table 4.1, however, does show some fluctuation in the levels of sales year on year. Clearly the policy took off spectacularly with over half a million dwellings sold in the first four years. Numbers did then tend to drop off slightly until another spurt after 1987, which coincided with the increase in discounts and reduction in qualifying periods introduced in the mid-1980s. The recession of the late 1980s and early 1990s saw a decline in sales but in the worst year (1996) the number was still very nearly 50,000. However, the following year saw a further increase which may have coincided with the election of the Labour government and some fears that the RTB might be restricted or even ended. The Labour government did undertake a review of the RTB and this led to the reduction in discounts in 1999. Perhaps of more significance to the figures was the shift in policy after 2000 towards stock transfer. Again the fear that tenants would lose their right to buy if the stock was transferred (even though this did not happen to existing tenants) might have encouraged the spike in sales between 2002 and 2004. As we discussed at the top of the chapter, the RTB has now declined quite considerably with the data for 2008 apparently showing a decline of 85% on the figure of just less than 25,000 in 2007. This suggests that total sales for 2008 would be below 5,000. The longer qualifying periods introduced in 2005 would also have had some effect in reducing numbers. We shall discuss the issue of the RTB's decline in more detail later in the chapter, as well as considering whether the RTB still has a future.

But even if the RTB is now exhausted, the data in Table 4.1 show the considerable impact it has had. This becomes even clearer when we look at data on changes in tenure between 1981 and 2006 as detailed in Table 4.2. This shows the changes in the main housing tenures in the various constituent parts of Great Britain. These data show that owner occupation has increased markedly since the introduction of the RTB and the local authority stock has declined by an even greater extent. This latter phenomenon was caused by the RTB, but also by stock transfer (which partly accounts for the growth of housing associations along with the fact that all new social house building has been in this sector). The decline in council housing is most marked in Scotland where only 35% of the stock level of 1981 remains (as opposed to 43.5% in England) even though it remains a higher proportion of the total stock. Perhaps this explains the more restrictive policies of the Scottish government we considered in Chapter 3.

We should note that even though the stock of housing association dwellings has increased (and by nearly 400% at that) this has not been sufficient to offset the decline in council housing. The two sectors combined totalled 31.2% in 1981 compared with only 18.5% in 2006. This demonstrates quite markedly that the Conservatives' desire to break the influence of council housing was successful. The political effect of this is that social housing, even

Table 4.2: Tenure changes, 1981–2006 (%)

	1981	2006
England		
Owner occupation	59.8	70.2
Private renting	11.3	11.9
Housing association	2.3	8.4
Local authority	26.6	9.5
Scotland		
Owner occupation	36.4	67.1
Private renting	9.7	7.4
Housing association	1.8	10.5
Local authority	52.1	15.1
Wales		
Owner occupation	61.9	72.7
Private renting	9.6	10.4
Housing association	2.2	5.0
Local authority	26.4	11.9
Great Britain		
Owner occupation	57.7	70.1
Private renting	11.1	11.4
Housing association	2.2	8.4
Local authority	29.0	10.1

Source: Wilcox (2008)

in Scotland where it was once the majority tenure, is now politically negligible. We shall discuss the residualisation of social housing in more detail below and look at the contribution that the RTB made to this, but it is clear that the Conservative aim of ending what it saw as 'the feudal system of municipal housing' (Conservative Party, 1976, p 15) was put well on the way by the RTB.

It was not just that tenants had the right to buy their dwelling that mattered, but that they could do so at a discount. This meant the housing was considerably cheaper than buying on the open market and so opened up the possibility of ownership to a much wider group of people. Table 4.3 shows the average levels of discounts for the English regions for a 10–year period up to 2008 (this type of data was not collected prior to 1998). What this shows, and we have to presume that the period before 1998 was little different, is that the average RTB claimant received a considerable discount of around 50%. This suggests that most tenants were long-standing council tenants with 50% discount equating to 20 years' occupancy of a house under the original 1981 regulations. The average might equate to only five years for flat dwellers after 1996 but, as we shall see below, flats only made up around a third of sales at most in any one year. This presumption on length of residency is important for two reasons. First, it shows a lack of opportunism in that these residents did not take up a tenancy merely to buy the dwelling. Second, length of tenure also indicates a commitment to the dwelling and the surrounding area. These households had put down roots and were not seeking to leave their home or their neighbourhood. This is an important point about the RTB that is often neglected: buying a dwelling on a council estate shows commitment to the locality, not contempt for it. This is a point we shall return to in the discussion below.

Discount levels were slightly higher in London, perhaps due to the relative scarcity of affordable alternative sources of housing in the capital. However, it is in London that restrictions in discounts have had the greatest effect with the average discount dropping to only 13% in 2007/08, despite the fact that the level of maximum discount remains higher.

Table 4.3: Average RTB discounts as a percentage of market value (English regions)

	98/99	99/00	00/01	01/02	02/03	03/04	04/05	05/06	06/07	07/08
North East	48	47	47	46	45	42	34	34	31	28
North West	48	48	47	46	45	43	41	37	34	32
Yorks & Humberside	47	47	46	46	44	43	40	35	31	28
East Mids	50	46	45	43	41	38	35	31	28	27
West Mids	49	48	49	47	44	40	34	33	30	30
Eastern	49	47	45	43	39	35	33	30	27	25
London	53	51	48	42	37	32	28	22	14	13
South East	50	47	44	42	39	35	32	30	28	26
South West	50	48	46	44	40	36	34	31	28	27
England	50	48	47	44	41	37	33	31	27	24

Source: www.publications.parliament.uk/pa/cm200708/cmhansrd/cm080910/text/80910w0048.htm (accessed 5 March 2009). Data only collected after 1998.

A further important point shown by the level of discount is that the amounts of capital receipts going to local authorities were limited to only half the market value. Likewise, the reduction in discounts indicates that over time the level of useable capital receipts increased and the financial incentives shifted more towards the local authority. This links back to the issue at the top of this chapter about the financial consequences of the decline of the RTB. Local authorities were receiving higher receipts per dwelling even though overall numbers were smaller.

The type of properties sold under the RTB was also important. Jones and Murie (2006) show that in England between 1981 and 1987 over 90% of dwellings sold per annum were houses. This began to alter after changes to discounts for flats in 1986, but even in the best year they report (1991) flats only made up 36.8% of dwellings sold. Jones and Murie show that by 1991 in England 44% of semi-detached family houses had been sold, compared to 18% of smaller terraced houses and 7% of flats. This has had consequences for local authorities, as we shall see, in that the RTB was introduced as local authorities were taking on the responsibility to house homeless families. Councils were left with fewer suitable dwellings to help these families just as the demand was increasing. This, as we shall see, is one of the key concerns with regard to the RTB – that local authorities were left with fewer tools to do their job properly – but the actual situation is rather more complex than is often suggested.

In the rest of this chapter I want to discuss some of the detailed issues regarding the impact of the RTB. Some of these relate to the scale of the policy and these have been signposted earlier. However, there are other issues that relate to the principle of the RTB rather than the scale of its impact. Some of the discussion is hypothetical or speculative, such as what would have happened without the RTB and how far the RTB has contributed to the residualisation of social housing. However, this does not mean that the discussion is not important or significant. Indeed, there is no choice but to speculate on these issues as we have no alternative RTB-free universe to compare with our own world. What makes the discussion more relevant is that opponents of the RTB use these very same hypothetical arguments to criticise the RTB.

What difference did it make?

One particularly interesting speculation is to ask what would have happened without the RTB. Would the so-called 'golden age' of council housing have persisted without the RTB? Might social housing have thrived and remained a normal tenure, providing people with a wider choice of options rather than the necessity of owner occupation? Most obviously we can suggest that there would have been no change in stock numbers, at least not until the advent of stock transfer in the 1990s. Instead of the depleted stock of 2.6 million there would still be nearer the 1981 figure of 6.1 million. This would have meant that councils would have had greater opportunity to house the homeless and to meet urgent housing need.

Yet this argument is to accept precisely the criticism that Jones and Murie (2006) make about the Conservatives: it is to see the RTB in isolation and to assume that it is the sole cause of the residualisation of social housing. It is to presume that the other important changes of the 1970s and 1980s did not also take place, such as the cuts in expenditure, stock transfer, the use of private finance by housing associations, the increased uptake of Housing Benefit and statutory homelessness increasingly becoming the primary route into the tenure. The RTB, therefore, only formed one part of the transformation of social housing.

We must assume that the impact of homelessness and Housing Benefit dependency would have been as significant. Indeed, it is highly likely that the problems of worklessness would have been greater if more homeless and economically dependent households had been housed. Likewise, even without the RTB we must presume that the spending reductions of the 1980s and 1990s would still have occurred, which would have meant still no new building. If we wished to return to the pre-RTB state we would therefore have to assume that many other things did not change as well. This might have been the case if Labour had won the elections in 1979 or 1983, but we shall never know.

A related argument about the RTB is to state that 2.5 million dwellings have been somehow lost. These dwellings are no longer available to social housing and so it is taken for granted that they have gone. However, these dwellings remain occupied and used, and their inherent utility in meeting the housing needs of the country as a whole is in no way diminished. The properties therefore have not gone anywhere.

What critics of the RTB mean by dwellings being lost, of course, is that they are no longer available for social housing tenants, and so landlords cannot use these dwellings to meet what they determine to be priority need. But this argument is only deemed significant if social housing is taken in isolation and seen in a narrow focus, something, to reiterate, that the Conservatives were criticised for in 1979/80.

It is crucial to any understanding of the RTB to remember that the households who bought their dwellings did not move away. Accordingly, they did not lose contact with their neighbours, but stayed precisely where they were and maintained the same relationships. This ought to be an obvious point, although it does tend to be overlooked by those who talk of 'lost' properties.

Of course, it might have been the case, as some anecdotes suggest, that the attitudes of RTB households towards their neighbours changed and they became less tolerant. However, this presumes that RTB households were isolated amongst a sea of tenants, which was often not the case, certainly by the end of the 1980s. But we also need to ask why we necessarily see it as a bad thing for one household to complain about another. Surely it depends on the particular situation, and to suggest that RTB households have become less tolerant is perhaps to be guilty of a prejudice against those who have acted in a manner one disapproves of. It is, after all, only the critics of the RTB who make this point about lack of tolerance.

We cannot argue that RTB households opted out of their estates. Indeed, we might argue that they actually did the opposite, in that they invested much more in their area, through their long-term financial commitment to their dwelling and the fact that they were now expected to take greater responsibility for their dwelling and its immediate environs. So we might say that they have invested much more in their area and dwelling than social tenants ever could. Not only have they chosen to remain there, but they have invested financially in the dwelling.

However, this is often not recognised, and even the opposite assumption is made, namely, that RTB households have taken much out of the system, in the form of their discount, but given nothing back. There is an assumption that because they are no longer social tenants they are selfish and show no solidarity, as if social tenants are themselves particularly solidaristic simply because of who their landlord is. We might be able to argue that the process that houses people in need is demonstrative of social solidarity, but this says nothing about the people who are housed as a result, nor does it predict how they will behave.

Likewise, it is not possible to suggest that the RTB shows there to be any problem with the housing itself. Why would households commit their own money to a dwelling that they did not like in an area they cared little for? Rather we can suggest that the RTB says more about the tenure of social housing, and particularly the management of the dwellings and relationship the landlord had with households in legal and financial terms. In terms of the reasons for buying, the issue was around who owned and controlled the dwelling. The RTB was not a comment on the housing – or at least not in a negative sense; we might, though, see it as positive – but on the ownership of the dwelling and the conditions of access and use applied by the owner on the tenant. The RTB took households into what we might call – with some due caution – the mainstream. The RTB transformed an unequal relationship based on supplication and dependency on the decisions of others, into the norm of a property-owning and responsible household. It turned people from being exceptions, who had to be helped, or were perceived as such, to people who were now free-standing.

We should not underplay this aspect of the RTB. The Conservatives saw owner occupation as inculcating independence and personal responsibility and of offering something that we could call 'ours'. We might argue whether ownership actually has this effect and whether we risk turning owner occupation into a fetish. Also we might suggest that property ownership is an ideological construct and so carries nothing that is intrinsic (Jacobs et al, 2003; Ronald, 2008).[2] Yet the practical perception of the benefits of owner occupation was what actually affected behaviour. A majority of individuals, at least before the credit crunch of 2008, believed in the superiority of owner occupation and took it as the normal tenure. The RTB allowed millions of households to act upon this perception.

But there is a further argument that we need to consider when speculating on what might or might not have changed. One key criticism of the RTB is that the dwellings sold were no longer available for re-letting to those in priority need. But this ignores the very obvious point that none of these dwellings were empty and available for re-let (Ward, 1985). These dwellings were fully occupied by definition and many of these tenants had been in occupation for many years and so we could not expect them to have moved in short order if the RTB had not existed. We might also argue that the fact that these tenants bought their dwelling and so made a considerable financial commitment to it is indicative of a desire to stay there. We can therefore not assume that these dwellings would have been available even in the long term. So, on one level, we can argue that if the RTB had not happened the same people would be living in the same houses!

Of course, over time re-lets would have arisen as tenants died, or left, and so eventually the RTB would have had some impact on availability. But exactly how much is speculative, as we cannot know how many of these dwellings would have become vacant, and therefore any argument is dependent on assumptions which cannot be tested. Clearly the RTB would have had some effect on availability, as commentators like Jones and Murie (2006) have sought to suggest. The reduction not just in overall numbers but in larger family houses would have had an impact on the ability of social landlords to meet local housing need. But there is by no means a direct and quantifiable relationship to state that the RTB created an increase in homelessness. As we shall see later in this chapter, the increase in homelessness in the 1980s was as much a function of changing priorities as the RTB, and the fact that homelessness has increased and decreased over the last 20 years demonstrates this (Wilcox, 2008).

Who was it for?

The RTB helped working-class households achieve what most academics and other middle-class professionals take for granted: owning their own home. It did this by keeping existing communities intact, which itself is a key aim of much housing policy over the last 30 years. We would have thought, then, that the policy would have received some support from those seeking to represent the interests of working-class people and the communities they are part of. Indeed, as we have seen, there are some representatives of the left who have supported the RTB, for example, the former Labour minister, Frank Field. He has supported the sale of council houses since the 1970s (Field, 1976), but with the key difference that receipts would be kept and used to replace the stock. Field sees letting working-class people gain access to owner occupation, with the benefit of inculcating personal responsibility, as a form ethical socialism consistent with the traditional roots of the Labour Party. This is perhaps a minority position on the left, but it does show that there is nothing necessarily right-wing about the RTB. Indeed, as we have seen, there are those on the right who argue against the RTB as an unreasonable intervention in markets. For some on the right there are no reasons that justify subsidising owner occupation.

There is actually some suggestion that Mrs Thatcher was at one time opposed to the idea of council house sales. Green (2006) states that she initially opposed the RTB in the early 1970s and only came to support it after she became leader. The reason for this, Green argues, is the two election defeats in 1974 and the need to rebuild a base of support for the Conservatives. Thatcher felt that there was a need to extend the property-owning democracy and to show that the Conservatives were in touch with the aspirations of the working classes. The Conservatives saw owner occupation as being popular, even amongst Labour supporters, and the RTB was therefore a means of capitalising on this latent desire.

According to Green, the RTB had clear targets:

> The sale of council houses, coupled with the government's refusal to allow local authorities to use the receipts from sales to finance new municipal housing, was designed to reduce the socio-geographical environment of Labourism, and to reconstruct the nature of important sections of the urban working class constituency in order to render it more receptive to Thatcherite Conservative values. Thatcher sought not merely to reflect the wishes of the electorate, but to *shape* that electorate and its wishes. (2006, p 130, original emphasis)

Green suggests that as the Conservative vote fell in the 1980s, this aim did not succeed. Higher levels of owner occupation did not make the Conservatives the natural party of government or condemn the Labour Party to everlasting exile. What did change, however, was the creation of a property-owning democracy. Green states that: 'What (the RTB) may have done was to consolidate gains the party had already made among the skilled working class in 1979' (2006, p 130). Likewise, the change in the Labour Party's position to support of the RTB by the 1987 General Election did not make them any more electable. Perhaps we should see the RTB, and owner occupation more generally, as being part of the normal cultural conditions that most had come to accept and expect (King, 2006a), and it was necessary for the Labour Party to show that it understood these expectations. Hence the RTB can stand alongside iconic policies of the last 30 years such as keeping income tax levels low and controlling the actions of trade unions as measures necessary for any political party to be taken seriously by the electorate.

There has, of course, been a considerable debate in the literature (summarised effectively by Saunders, 1990) on the relationship between tenure and voting behaviour, and a considerable amount of the debate has centred on the effect of the RTB in creating a constituency for the Conservatives amongst erstwhile Labour supporters. But this is now to a considerable extent an irrelevance, particularly after three election defeats for the Conservatives since 1997. Perhaps what we might now argue is that owner occupation has developed to such an extent that all parties support this tenure and so it has become rather more neutral in its electoral impact.[3]

The discussion so far suggests that there were a number of beneficiaries of the RTB. First, there were 2.5 million households who exercised their statutory right. These were households who aspired to ownership and had the necessary resources and capability once given sufficient encouragement. We might see these as a minority, albeit a significant one. However, as we have stated it is difficult to point to many other housing policies that have had anything like the same impact.

Second, we can suggest that the Conservative governments might have benefited in terms of increasing or maintaining their popularity such that they could win four consecutive elections. But the RTB also helped them greatly in their attempts to curb the role and influence of local governments. The RTB had a particularly close fit with the Conservatives' political and ideological agenda.

Third, and perhaps more controversially, the country as a whole can be said to have benefited, in terms of creating more people with a stake in a social system based on individual property rights. The RTB helped the spread of owner occupation and the perception of affluence more widely, creating higher levels of personal responsibility and stability as a result. Of course, those who oppose the RTB might point to greater social division as a result, but this argument depends on looking at the issue of owner occupation from the perspective of the shrinking minority rather than the growing majority. We might equally argue that a dominant tenure is a sign of cohesion rather than division.

Fourth, and again perhaps contentiously, we might state that the RTB led to a general improvement of the housing stock through greater private investment and care by owners compared with the maintenance and management of social landlords. The RTB was undertaken at a time when the resources available to social landlords were in decline and dwellings were not modernised and maintained according to modern standards.[4]

Indeed, one group we have not yet considered is social landlords, those who effectively had a duty to sell their properties. We can suggest that their interests have not been best served by the RTB. As was shown by the limited success of voluntary sales schemes in the 1970s, most social landlords did not wish to sell their dwellings. Quite naturally they have argued that the sale of dwellings has had a considerable impact on their ability to deal with local housing need. As we have seen, not only did they lose over 2.5 million dwellings in aggregate, but this number included a disproportionate amount of their larger family properties which would help them rehouse the homeless. In this regard, we should remember that even though local authorities have lost nearly 40% of their dwellings due to the RTB (plus a further 20% to stock transfer), they have not lost any of their statutory responsibilities towards the homeless and meeting housing need in their area.

However, to balance this, a considerable proportion of the funding for council housing was provided by central government, and so we might argue that it was quite legitimate for an elected government to change things, especially if it had a manifesto commitment to do so. Of course, this boils down to a debate on who best represents the community or the 'social', and where authority and legitimacy lies within the British state. It is perhaps relevant in this regard that the statutory responsibilities of local authorities arise out of Acts of Parliament promulgated by central government. The statutory responsibility to help the homeless has therefore the same status as, and no more than, the statutory Right to Buy.

We also need to question how far the structural and financial integrity of several hundred local authorities weighs against the interests of millions of households. In what sense can we argue that one interest is deemed to be more important than another? Perhaps one way of dealing with this is to state that organisations have an instrumental quality, whilst households, being made up of individual human beings, have an intrinsic one. Local authorities, like all institutions created by human design are means to an end, and this end is the flourishing of individuals and communities. The organisational or structural integrity of local authorities cannot be allowed to outweigh the interests of human beings.

Of course, we might argue that the RTB has prevented social landlords from fulfilling their role to ensure that some flourish. We have already dealt with this issue in part, with the practical argument that these dwellings were not and would not necessarily have become empty even in the long term. But on a more principled level, we need to assess in what way the rights of one group outweigh the interests of another. Why do the rights of future tenants, whom the landlord may be unaware of, trump those of its current tenants? All housing policies are competitive, in that they involve the allocation of resources in conditions of scarcity. There is then a debate over whose rights should triumph, and the means that are used in most developed countries is the popular will. On this basis we would have to argue that a sitting tenant's right to buy was, and is, seen as superior to that of a prospective homeless person or the property rights of social landlords.

The reason that the RTB has been so controversial is, of course, precisely that there are other demands placed on social landlords and the RTB has exacerbated their ability to fulfil the full range of their responsibilities in the manner they would perhaps have liked. As a result it is easy to lay the blame on the RTB and state that if it had not been present then other problems would have either disappeared or been much less severe. But why, we might ask, is it always assumed that the cause of the problem is the RTB? Why is the problem not caused by other policies?

Was it the RTB's fault?

Some housing policies are seen as beneficial, whilst others are viewed negatively. This means that some policies are welcomed and campaigners and commentators might call for more of them (building more housing, higher standards of amenity and so on), but others, it is argued, should be repealed or ended. Of course, there is no necessary consensus on what is considered good or bad. However, we can generalise somewhat and suggest that the balance of academic opinion is that the RTB falls into the 'bad' category. What tends to happen as a result is that the RTB is blamed for much of the decline of social housing, whilst other policies are viewed either as being neutral or having a positive impact.

It is therefore instructive to look at three policies which can be said to have had a fundamental impact on the current configuration of social housing. The first policy is the RTB itself, and it should be clear to us what impact it has had in terms of numbers and the type of properties sold. The other two policies are statutory homeless provision and Housing Benefit.

In 1974 a comprehensive system of housing allowances was introduced to help those on low incomes pay their rent. The importance of this change was that the ability to pay rent was no longer an obstacle to accessing council housing. So for the first time in its history council housing was accessible to the very poorest. Provisions to assist certain homeless households were introduced in

1977, giving priority access to social housing to families with children. Many of these households, because of the nature of the access route, were dependent on benefits and were vulnerable.

These two policies altered the demographic of social housing, opening it up to households who were poorer and more vulnerable than had been typical prior to the 1970s. The RTB, of course, had the reverse effect of taking the more affluent tenants out of the sector. These tenants took their dwellings with them, which, as we have seen, were the larger family dwellings. The overall result has been the residualisation of social housing, with two thirds of tenants dependent on benefits and only a minority in paid employment (Hills, 2007). However, only one of these policies is criticised: there is a conspicuous lack of critics calling for the abolition of the homeless legislation and Housing Benefit. Critics tend to argue rather for their extension.

We can speculate on which of these policies has had the greatest effect, but it is impossible to disentangle one from the other in any complete way. Social housing is open and dynamic in its operation and so we cannot isolate any one policy (King, 2009). Rather, these three policies interacted in a non-systematic manner over a long period of time and in a way that was complicated and uneven.

This being so, why should we assume that the RTB has had a greater negative effect? This is particularly so as we can suggest that the RTB did not cause the change in the make-up of social tenants, this being due to homelessness and the availability of Housing Benefit. Moreover, the RTB was the last of the three policies to be introduced and so the other two were already having their impact. In any case, as we have seen, RTB households remained committed to the same dwellings and stayed relatively independent of state intervention. Accordingly, we might characterise the cause of residualisation as being the fact that whilst the more affluent households were leaving via the RTB route, those entering social housing were not working families, but were rather from priority-need groups who were predominantly dependent on benefits.

But we can compare the RTB with more recent policies. Local authorities have lost over 970,000 dwellings through stock transfer to the housing association sector (Wilcox, 2008). Since 2000 this has largely been imposed by central government as a means of levering in private finance to fund stock improvements (King, 2009). But what, we might ask, does the policy of stock transfer imply about the perceived competence of local authorities? There is clearly another agenda here, about using private finance and private organisations, but the policy does show that there is only a limited commitment to the idea of public sector support for vulnerable households. This commitment has been privatised through stock transfer, just as the RTB privatised a large body of dwellings. Of course, it can be argued that the transferred stock remains available for renting, which is true, but the policy cannot be presented as any sort of endorsement for the role of local authorities.

The same applies to policies to encourage low-cost home ownership (LCHO), which received a boost by government in 2007 (CLG, 2007). This involves the use of government funding, which would otherwise be used by social landlords to maintain or increase their stock, to subsidise owner occupation for certain groups of key workers or low-income households on local authority housing lists. We might have thought that it would be difficult for landlords to accept funding to develop these sorts of schemes but then oppose the RTB which uses public assets to fund owner occupation for low-income groups. We might say that LCHO does not reduce the stock of social dwellings, yet this would not be strictly true. As we have stated already, RTB dwellings were not empty and would not have been available for re-letting. On the other hand, government subsidies used for LCHO have definitely reduced the amount of funding available for new social dwellings.

Likewise, the Decent Homes Standard, aimed at improving the quality of the social housing stock, has also had the effect of reducing the stock of new dwellings. This is because the government has made the improvement of existing stock a priority at the expense of new development. This very mechanistic policy, which forced social landlords to spend money on stock improvements whether they were strictly needed or not, meant that new social house building in the 2000s has been at the lowest level since the end of the Second World War.

So we can question how far the residualisation of social housing was due to the RTB. We might argue that residualisation was happening in any case because of the effects of Housing Benefit and homelessness, allied to the spending reductions which began under the Callaghan government in 1976. The problem with social housing became one of a concentration of benefit-dependent households, where working households no longer counted because they either had bought their dwelling or could no longer gain access because of priority need. The function and role of social housing had already begun to change before the RTB, and was only sped up by it.

One key problem in any discussion on social housing is that its supporters tend to believe it has either a neutral or positive impact on tenants. There is a general refutation of behavioural explanations – that certain modes of provision create dependency – and hence there is no recognition that social housing alters behaviour. However, there is no such reticence in ascribing particular types of behaviour to those who desire to own, especially if it is their council house.

But it is clear that the manner in which social housing interacts with low-income households does alter behaviour. What has altered since the 1970s is the means of accessing social housing and the expectations placed on those who succeed. In both the 1970s and the present we can suggest that the key issue is access and how this is organised. However, in the 1970s the main means of rationing access was by date-order waiting lists, and so what mattered was a degree of patience to wait in turn, some persistence to remain on the list and keep one's situation up-to-date, and to conform to certain norms of behaviour. However, once one had gained access, as long as one paid the rent on time and adhered to the tenancy regulations, one could then expect very limited contact with the landlord. The expectation of the landlord and tenant was that they behaved in the same manner as they had when on the waiting list, and in this sense there was very little difference between those who were tenants and those who were not.

However, there is now a considerable difference between social tenants and those outside the tenure. Partly this is due to the change in the relative size of the two sectors due to the decline of social renting. But we can also point to other factors. First, to become a tenant often necessitates making one's condition as bad as possible, by having a low or, even better, no income, by being seen as vulnerable (and there are now helpful definitions to work towards), by being homeless (again according to the official definition) and so on. Acting according to the norms of traditional behaviour before gaining a tenancy, such as waiting to start a family or even forming a household, is now to disadvantage oneself and will almost certainly mean that one will not be granted a tenancy. Means-tested access rather than date-order queuing insists that one needs to maximise one's problems rather than minimising them.

Second, this situation persists once a tenancy is granted, because of the situation of the household, who will need financial support in the form of welfare benefits including Housing Benefit. So means testing is maintained and the incentive to maximise entitlements remains. Third, this means that the relationship with the landlord and the state remains one of continual intervention and support, particularly financially.

This creates a perpetual distinction between tenants and non-tenants: one becomes a tenant initially by not fulfilling the norms of society – and the term 'socially excluded' is particularly apposite here, although perhaps not in the manner intended – and one is encouraged by circumstances and means testing to persist with this segregation once one becomes a tenant. To act like a responsible member of society – paying one's own bills from one's private income – is more risky and onerous and militates against the manner by which one has been granted access to social housing. What this suggests is that there is a structural deficiency inherent in social housing, in that the means of accessing and maintaining a tenancy encourage the persistence of economic dependency.

This brings us back to the question of what social housing would now be like were it not for the RTB, and particularly the question of whether social housing would have been sustainable at the level of over 6 million dwellings. In a situation like this we might speculate that the effects of benefit dependency and access via priority need would have been uncontainable. This being so, might we not argue that the RTB allowed successive governments to put off fundamental reform of social housing and Housing Benefit? The RTB allowed working households to gain an asset, whilst reducing the scale and size of the tenure. Hence social housing became less electorally significant and so could be ignored. According to this view, working households were 'bought off' by the RTB, whilst the poorest were pacified by the benefit system. However, the result is a dysfunctional and residualised social housing system. This explanation, as speculative as it is, is not intended to suggest any particular long-term plan for social housing on the part of past or present governments. All the policies we have discussed here were developed separately, at different times and with a specific purpose in mind. However, the overall effect of these policies has been the long-term residualisation of social housing.

The RTB has shown that the interests of working-class households do not lie necessarily within social housing. It has therefore helped to question the traditional role of social housing as working-class housing. The policy response, intended or otherwise, has been to alter fundamentally the nature of social housing away from being working-class housing to what we might now term *non-working-class housing*. The dominant groups in social housing are now those who are workless and dependent on welfare benefits.

This has the effect of broadening the polarity between those who have exercised their right to buy and those now seen as typical social tenants. As social housing is now taken as non-working-class housing the RTB is seen as even more problematical. We can see this distance by the rather perverse manner in which social landlords have been promoting owner occupation. Because social housing is lacking diversity and is dominated by the vulnerable, social landlords now attempt to introduce diversity by encouraging low-cost home ownership. What this shows, however, is that the only manner that working-class households can be drawn back into the orbit of social landlords is through owner occupation. Social landlords' notion of diversity is therefore to provide something other than social housing, namely, subsidised owner occupation, which, of course, is precisely what the RTB was. However, housing commentators maintain the fiction that LCHO is somehow a distinctive and sophisticated response to a lack of affordability, whilst the RTB is seen as illegitimate.

This development, whereby social landlords seek to create diversity through funding owner occupation, brings us back to one of the key points raised at the start of this chapter. Owning our own home is now taken as the norm, it is expected and forms the basis from which we judge housing policy. Just as local authorities are now dependent on the capital receipts from RTB sales, so is owner occupation the necessary state of affairs. This is now so embedded that social landlords find themselves promoting LCHO in an almost exact reversal of the RTB: one becomes an owner-occupier through a relationship with a social landlord instead of ending the association as was the case with the RTB.

But we might also see LCHO as an alternative to the RTB and one that takes up the slack as the RTB declines. The RTB has declined from the heyday of the early 1980s when well over 100,000 dwellings a year were sold to a figure for 2008 of perhaps below 5,000. In the final part of this chapter we therefore need to consider some of the reasons why the RTB has declined.

Where did it go?

Whilst the RTB is of great historical and symbolic importance, which probably ensures its survival, it is now certainly not particularly significant when compared with the effects of policies such as stock transfer. Since 2007 more social housing has been built than sold under the RTB, which means that the total stock is actually rising for the first time since 1981 (King, 2009). There are a number of reasons the RTB has declined.

First, we might argue that most of the typical purchasers – households with a steady and regular income – have already left social housing, often, of course, through taking advantage of the RTB. Second, as we have seen, allocation according to priority need has meant that these households were not replaced with similar households, but with ones more likely to be dependent on benefits and so unable to afford to buy.

A third reason is that the high level of take-up of the RTB has meant that there are now fewer attractive properties that households might seek to buy. In addition, very nearly all the family houses built since the late 1980s are owned by housing associations and let on assured tenancies where the RTB does not apply. Fourth, stock transfer has also meant that many more tenants have become assured tenants. Whilst those tenants transferring with the stock kept their existing rights, new ones went onto assured tenancies. Fifth, we might suggest that the restrictions on discounts and qualifying periods introduced since 1999 have reduced the attractiveness of the RTB.

All of these reasons have led to a steady decline in sales, but, as we saw at the start of this chapter, the collapse in the housing market and the credit crunch in 2008 have dramatically sped up the decline of the RTB. It might be that this leads to the end of the RTB. If it declines even further in 2009/10 and beyond it might provide government with an excuse to let it die. As we shall see in the next chapter, opportunist calls to suspend or end the RTB on the grounds of the housing collapse were given short shrift by the Brown government in late 2008. However, a refusal to abolish the RTB outright is not the same as refusing to allow the RTB to wither away.

Of course, much of this depends on the extent and longevity of the financial crisis facing Britain and the rest of the world. It might well be that the RTB makes something of a comeback as economic conditions improve. But were this to happen, the reasons for the steady decline since 1999 would still remain: most tenants are not in work and many are ineligible because they are now housing association tenants.

In this chapter we have sought to explore the RTB as a policy and to evaluate its impact. We have seen that this impact is indeed considerable, but that there is also a substantial degree of controversy attached to it. The RTB is disliked even as social landlords are dependent on it and are using government funding to promote other forms of owner occupation for low-income households. We have seen that it is difficult to separate the exact impact of the RTB from other policies. But this has not meant that the RTB is immune from criticism. Rather, as we shall see in the next chapter, most often consideration and criticism of the RTB are one and the same thing.

Notes

[1] I am particularly grateful here to the regular contributors to the Institute of Economic Affairs' blog for their comments on the RTB. Their responses have helped considerably in understanding the particular nuances of attitudes towards the RTB and owner occupation in general.

[2] I discuss the notion of the social construction of owner occupation in Chapter 5.

[3] This is a different thing from arguing that a government might suffer if it is seen as responsible for a fall in house prices, as in 1992–93 and 2008–09.

[4] It is interesting and informative that the priority of the Labour government after 2000 with regard to social housing was to improve the quality of the stock, through the Decent Homes Standard, rather than increase the size of the stock.

FIVE

What is wrong with it?

Introduction

It is not hard to find criticism of the Right to Buy (RTB). Indeed, to a large extent the literature on the RTB *is* criticism. The literature is perhaps the most unbalanced one could possibly imagine. Partly, this is because a lot of the literature comes from the early and mid-1980s when the main opposition party was still opposed to the policy and so there was some possibility of a return to the status quo. However, such a prospect ceased to be tenable once the Labour Party accepted the RTB after its landslide defeat in the 1983 election. But also the criticism derives from the particular aims of the RTB, namely, that it sought to attack social housing and promote owner occupation. Critics tend almost exclusively to focus on the effects of the RTB on other tenures and ignore the positive aim that the policy sought to have. This is a reverse image of the Conservatives who, as Jones and Murie (2006) have stated, focused solely on the aim of increasing owner occupation and did not countenance any negative impact on council housing. So we have two sides who are talking past each other, with different priorities and who cannot understand each other. We get a sense of this from looking at Williams (2003) and his summary of the RTB. His concern in this discussion was particularly on the manner in which governments since 1980 steadfastly refused to fund research on certain of the effects of the RTB. He is therefore able to conclude that:

> The history of the Right to Buy in Britain is not a happy one for those who believe that housing policy should be rational, based on evidence and with the objectives of maximising choice and quality in as fair a manner as possible. It began life as an ideological instrument to expand homeownership, which could be used as an electoral weapon, and rapidly became the single most effective revenue raiser for a government intent on swingeing cuts in public expenditure and personal taxation. (2003, p 245)

Williams is able to suggest that the policy is irrational, because it did not focus on the objectives he takes as important. Yet he sees that the RTB was also used by the government as a weapon to meet its aims, which might be taken by some as a sign of some sort of rational planning. Also the policy was both ideological *and* a cynical attempt to bolster revenues. This is quite a catalogue of criticisms for one policy.

Yet from the Conservatives' perspective, the evidence for the policy was clearly available in the form of the vast number of applicants each year. In this sense it also quite clearly met the objectives set for it, which were to expand owner occupation and to reduce the influence of local authorities over housing. It is hard to imagine more definitive evidence for the success of a policy.

But, of course, what Williams is critical of is that the government did not agree with his concerns and consider the effect that the RTB has on such matters as social landlords' ability to meet need and fulfil their obligations to the homeless, and the quality of housing left unsold. But why should a government, confident that a policy was doing what was intended of it, waste resources investigating other matters? To use Williams' word, why would this be rational? The problem, then, in considering reactions to the RTB is that its critics do not share the same ends as its proposers.

But how do we compare the different effects here? Is there some form of cost–benefit analysis we can use that allows us to weigh the benefits of an extra 2.5 million owner-occupiers against the effects on social housing, assuming, of course, we can actually determine what part of the residualisation of social housing was down to the RTB and what part to other policies? Does the net effect on society's ability to help the vulnerable outweigh the benefits of the RTB?

There is a very real problem of measurement here. How do we determine whether the RTB had a beneficial effect overall? Should it be measured in societal or individual terms, and how do we decide on this without already prejudging the merits of the social against the individual? Can we weigh the sum of individual satisfaction from purchasers against homeless households or those who might claim to have been kept on a waiting list for longer? Can we measure the encouragement of independence and personal responsibility against the increase in dependence? Can we calculate the amount of personal wealth creation? Is it possible to deal with changing expectations?

We might try to return to more practical questions. For example, are the problems with the RTB fundamental or systemic? Perhaps it is not the principle of the RTB itself which is at fault, but rather the manner in which it was implemented, with its discounts, right to a mortgage and the requirement of landlords to repay debt and offset subsidy entitlement, which meant that landlords could not replace their stock. Would the policy be easier to justify if it was not subsidised and dwellings were sold at market values, as some on the right have suggested? But these questions still turn on whether the effect of the creation of 2.5 million new owner-occupiers was more beneficial than the residualisation of social housing was detrimental.

We cannot escape from our normative starting point. Most critics of the RTB are supporters of social housing and this forms the basis of their criticism. Conversely most supporters of the RTB are so because they support the extension of owner occupation and wish to reduce government intervention. But this, in itself, raises some interesting counterfactuals. So, for example, would the RTB have been more acceptable to its critics if it had been introduced by Labour as Frank Field had argued in the 1970s (Field, 1976). Field linked the sale of council houses to the ideas of mutuality and self-help, which he saw as significant strands of socialism in the later 19th and early 20th centuries, but which were overwhelmed by state collectivism. Whilst we cannot know what might have happened if Field had been listened to in the 1970s, we can certainly suggest that the RTB appealed to the working class, to those households who were in secure jobs and who had historically been seen as the 'Labour aristocracy'. This group had been key Labour supporters, but had drifted away as they no longer saw Labour as matching their aspirations. Clearly, to become an owner-occupier was one of these aspirations.

It is also interesting that reducing the stock of housing for working-class households can actually be seen as beneficial if it is done for the right 'rational' reason and by the right people. For example, housing professionals and academics can be quite sanguine about the demolition of housing in so-called Housing Market Renewal Pathfinders, where apparently 'unwanted', but still occupied, housing is demolished and replaced by a smaller amount of so-called 'affordable housing' (King, 2006b). It is apparently acceptable to reduce the available housing stock for working-class households in places like Liverpool, Sheffield, Hull and Stoke, but not to sell council housing to sitting tenants in these cities. We can rip apart long-standing communities in order to make them 'sustainable' yet the RTB, which keeps communities intact and households in the dwellings they know, is reprehensible. Why is Housing Market Renewal taken to be a sophisticated and serious policy tool, making it legitimate to impose the demolition of dwellings on unwilling communities, whilst the RTB is deemed irrational? Clearly there is something complex at work here that relates to the ideology of social provision and attitudes towards private ownership.[1] Perhaps the key issue is that the RTB individualises housing, whilst policies such as Housing Market Renewal are socially configured. One policy is presumed to be based on individual interests whilst the others are centred on collectivist notions of the good, which justify overriding private interests through compulsory purchase and demolition.

It would be possible to build a case against the RTB by relying on critics like Williams. We could rehearse arguments about the increase in homelessness and whether this was caused by the RTB, or we could look in detail at the unfair nature of the subsidies going to RTB households compared with others. These issues will be discussed in this chapter, but I wish to concentrate also on more recent criticisms of the RTB rather than just these old debates. I choose to do this for a number of reasons.

First, there is much merit in concentrating on current issues especially as, at the time of writing (March 2009), the country is in recession and housing markets are severely depressed. Therefore, what is the place of the RTB and the support for owner occupation in a time of recession? The emphasis should now be on whether the RTB can be justified in what looks like the worst recession for over 70 years, when house prices are falling by over 17% per annum and when many households are finding it impossible to find a mortgage. We need to question just what it means to talk about 'the desire to own' when first-time buyers cannot get access to mortgage finance and the number of repossessions is increasing. Housing organisations are forecasting significant increases in the size of social landlords' waiting lists, and, if this is correct, should these same landlords still be forced to sell their dwellings to what are their least-deserving tenants; households who, it has to be said, were they to apply for social housing now would not be deemed a priority.

Second, I want to show that the nature of the criticism of the RTB is now largely dictated by the very success of the RTB and other owner-occupation initiatives. The recent criticisms are themselves based on the long-term effects of the RTB and the growth of owner occupation in general, and also show how the debate on housing tenure has been fundamentally shaped by policies such as the RTB. Criticism of the RTB has evolved and is now very much dependent on a set of circumstances which themselves are determined by attitudes towards owner occupation. These current criticisms did not arise out of a defence of social housing for itself, but rather in response to the crisis in housing markets in 2008–09. The recession, it is argued, means there may now be a heightened demand for social housing and so we should suspend or even end the RTB to help with this new demand. We need more social housing to support the housing market.

These policies, I want to suggest, show the complete victory of owner occupation and the conservative ideology that underpins it. It now seems only possible to attack the RTB as part of an avowed concern for housing markets and the need to support hard-pressed owners. These critics therefore use the current state of housing markets to attack one of the key means of extending owner occupation to working-class households. When this is coupled to the situation we considered in the previous chapter, of social landlords promoting diversity through low-cost home-ownership schemes, we can see that the desire to own is now so embedded it even forms a major plank of those wishing to promote social housing.

In this chapter we shall deal with a range of criticisms and seek to answer them. We shall consider what might be called the old criticisms of the RTB, those dating back to the 1980s, before moving on to look at perhaps the oldest of all, the notions of property ownership as false consciousness. However, we shall see how, in this post-Marxist age, this position has been modernised. We will then move on to consider some of the financial issues surrounding the RTB, although this will only be brief and there is no attempt to undertake a full financial analysis.

The chapter then considers what might be termed 'friendly fire', those criticisms from the right who see the RTB as social engineering or who see any form of subsidy to owner occupation as a skewing of market mechanisms. Finally, we turn to what might be seen as the new criticisms of the RTB brought on by the collapse of the housing market in 2008.

The case against

As I have suggested, the literature on the RTB is largely a series of criticisms. The issue for us now, 30 years after the policy was proposed, is just how we should deal with these criticisms. Many of these criticisms have gone largely unanswered, and so we might suggest that they need countering with some solid arguments in favour of the RTB. However, these ideas are well known and we might state that, as a result, they do not need much more of a hearing.

We also need to be aware that these critics have lost the argument, if the facts that the Conservatives managed to win four consecutive elections and their opponents were forced into changing their position on the RTB to one of support are of any significance. We can argue that the critique of the RTB has hardly impacted at all at the level of practical politics. If we were simply to content ourselves with the mainstream literature we would have no notion as to why the RTB succeeded and be left with a completely false impression.

This might lead us to conclude that these arguments might now be safely ignored. However, it might well be instructive to consider just why all these criticisms have been so ineffectual. The consistency of arguments by academics and commentators, and the opposition of the housing profession, has not dented the progress of the RTB. Indeed, even an avowedly hostile Secretary of State such as John Prescott, who was nominally in charge of housing policy for most of the Blair years, felt unable to do more than reduce discounts and lengthen qualifying periods. One of the key elements we need to explain is why a policy that is so derided by all the so-called experts has been immune to abolition and has had such an effect over such a long period.

We should therefore pay some attention to the main criticisms of the RTB that have been around for almost as long as the policy itself, even if just to understand why they have failed to have any impact. Balchin (1995) provides a convenient summary of these criticisms, showing how many were being made actually before the legislation was enacted. He states that the claims made by the Conservatives regarding the financial advantages of the RTB to the local and national tax-payers were over-optimistic and that the RTB actually caused hardship for local authorities in the form of lost rent income and did not reduce income support payments to tenants, as, by definition, those on benefits could not afford to buy. The policy favoured tenants on higher incomes and so disadvantaged the poorest who were unable to make a capital gain. However, Balchin also states that some purchasers found themselves in financial difficulties if their circumstances changed, or because of the cost of repairs and maintenance. He mentions that, from the age profile of buyers, many households would still be paying off their mortgages after retirement.

Having dealt with the issue of who bought, Balchin turns to what was bought. He makes the same point as that of Jones and Murie (2006), which we discussed in the last chapter, that the best properties were bought, leaving councils to soldier on with fewer large family houses and more unpopular flats. In addition, he points out that many rural authorities were left unable to deal with housing need in their areas due to the depletion of stock.

Balchin is also critical of the ability of purchasers to sell their dwellings for their full market price without any remittance after only a relatively short period of time. Any capital gain remained untaxed and so these former tenants were able to make a considerable gain at the tax-payers' expense. However, the government after 1981 did not allow local authorities the freedom to use their capital receipts on the grounds that this large amount of extra capital spending would be inflationary and defeat the government's spending plans. Since 1990 local authorities have been forced to use 75% of their receipts to pay off debt and so can only use 25% for new activity. This control over capital receipts has allowed central government both to reduce the net public borrowing requirement and reduce its capital allocations to local authorities. However, the effect of this is that councils have not greatly benefited financially from the sale of their assets.

Of course, we need to offset this last point with the discussion in Chapter 4 on the effect of the decline in RTB sales. Local authorities now actually do seem to appreciate, and have come to depend on, the level of receipts they have received. It is nevertheless true that much of the receipts have not been available to local authorities.

The arguments presented by Balchin can be seen as a comprehensive condemnation of the RTB, and we can see what Williams (2003) may have been talking about when he considered the policy to be irrational. But we have to remember that these arguments did not persuade the Conservatives or the electorate to change their positions, or prevent the Labour Party from changing its position in the mid-1980s. One of the reasons for this is that, as Williams has pointed out, many of these problems did not become evident for several years, even though they had been predicted. As all the dwellings were tenanted at the point of sale, there was no immediate loss of dwellings. Likewise, any significant loss in income would only become apparent once a reasonable number of dwellings had been sold. Williams also makes the point that bringing together much of this evidence needed the active help and funding of the government, which was not particularly forthcoming.

But, as I have stated earlier, the Conservatives saw no need to collect this sort of evidence because the RTB was doing what was intended of it. Hence the argument returns to the problem of competing normative positions. Accordingly, it is not that the Conservatives had particular answers to these criticisms of the RTB. Rather they felt that the benefits of the RTB outweighed the problems. What makes this controversial, of course, is that the benefits were enjoyed by one group, whilst the problems fell on others. However, it was this disjuncture that meant that the policy could work. The benefits and costs were out of phase with each other and those who benefitted were separated from the problems.

A key issue here is that those who benefited were individual households, who could vote, pay taxes and so on, whilst those who suffered were largely organisations. As we have discussed in Chapter 4, there is a significant difference in the manner in which individuals and organisations are to be treated morally. It might be argued that the fact that organisations such as social landlords were hampered had a knock-on effect for other individuals, such as those who could not be housed or who had to live in older and smaller dwellings. However, we need to remember that many households who gained a tenancy after 1981, despite perhaps waiting longer, also bought their dwellings.

What this suggests is that there is a distinction to be made here between a collectivist view of housing and an individualist one. The critics of the RTB see the policy in collectivist terms and accordingly dwell on generalities and abstractions, such as measures of housing standards, aggregates of dwellings and finance. However, for each household that bought, and for each one that aspired to, theirs was an individual decision based on their desires and aspirations. There was nothing abstract in this, but rather a determination to develop the specific relation with *their* dwelling. Once we appreciate this we can begin to see why it was that the RTB held the appeal it did, and why the criticisms of the policy could be overridden with such ease. Organisational interests could not – and should not – outweigh the material interests of individuals. It was this aspect of the RTB that allowed for its success, and, as we shall see in the next chapter, what makes it so special in public policy.

These arguments, I am sure, will not convince the RTB's critics, who will see the problems outlined earlier as unanswerable. However, we have dealt with some of the specific criticisms in Chapter 4, when we considered the causes of the residualisation of social housing. But, many critics will still be unconvinced, not because of specific arguments, but rather because they choose to weigh the collective and the abstract interest above those of individuals. The point about the RTB is not really whether it had the detrimental effects on other tenures claimed of it, but whether those effects outweigh the benefits.

The 'myth' of property ownership

The distinction between the collective and the individual also plays a significant part in more theoretical criticisms of the RTB. For example, Kemeny (1981; 2005) refers to the manner in which the urban built form creates distinctions between public and private choices. He sees rhetoric in support of owner occupation as a 'privatising discourse'. It is what he calls a hegemonic discourse which linked the growth of owner occupation to rising living standards and affluence. He is therefore able to talk of the 'myth' of owner occupation, as something that is socially constructed to create and maintain a position of social dominance by certain elements within society. For Kemeny, the promotion of owner occupation promotes private choices at the expense of collective or public ones.

This notion of social constructs and hegemonic discourses, of course, has its roots in Marxist notions of false consciousness. In Chapter 2 we saw how critics like Honderich (1990) have argued that property ownership merely favours one particular class. He states that 'the conservative society ... enlarges the total of what is distributed according to the ability to pay and decreases the total of what is distributed according to need' (1990, p 89). He sees property ownership as a zero–sum game, where allowing the few to gain more deprives the majority from realising their desires. He suggests that 'the conservative desire and strategy to increase to a limited extent the number of holders of some small amount of property, notably a home or a few shares' does not carry 'the great benefits of other amounts and forms of property' (p 93). Owner occupation does not, Honderich seems to believe, allow these individuals to accumulate capital, and they are therefore not part of the property-owning class in the classical Marxist sense. Increasing levels of owner occupation, according to Honderich, therefore merely creates the illusion of being part of a propertied class.

As we saw in Chapter 2, this argument is essentially patronising of the capabilities of those very working people whose interests socialists like Honderich claim to be protecting and promoting. It seeks to criticise owner occupation through demeaning those who have taken advantage of it. This is, as we shall see, a common argument for those trying to explain how owner occupation can be so bad, and yet so popular. Those on the left have long had to deal with the problem of why those they claim to be supporting insist on rejecting them.

Again, we might see these arguments as being largely discredited. However, there are two reasons for looking at these notions. First, the collapse in the housing market in 2007/08 has led to a questioning of the often unspoken virtues of owner occupation, with even academics from the right questioning whether it should be relied upon (Ferguson, 2008). It might, therefore, be opportune to reopen some of the old debates about the nature of property ownership. Second, the newer notions of discourse and social construction have developed some currency in housing research and so they are arguments we should take seriously. Indeed, they are ostensibly different and more sophisticated than the rather blunt arguments of Honderich.

So whilst Marxist ideas have tended to disappear from the mainstream of housing studies over the last couple of decades, we can see an increasing use of discourse analysis, which makes use of the idea of *hegemony* developed largely by the Italian Marxist thinker, Gramsci (1971). Hegemony can be described as the 'common sense' world view of the dominant class that is successfully imposed on a society. However, the notion need not carry with it any of the essentialist arguments that plagued Marxist ideas in the 1960s and 1970s associated with thinkers such as Althusser (1968) and Castells (1977). Instead, hegemony can be linked to post-structuralist concepts of the self and identity to explore the manner in which ideology is embedded within all social relations (Laclau, 1993; Zizek, 1999).

Ideology, according to these theorists, is manifested in discourse. The analysis of discourse, according to Torfing (1999), offers an anti-essentialist view of the individual subject as constantly constructed and reconstructed socially:

> In sharp contrast to the essentialist conception of identity, discourse analysis emphasises the construction of social identity in and through

hegemonic practices of articulation, which partially fixes the meaning
of social identities by inscribing them in the differential system of a
certain discourse. (p 41)

What this means is that the subject is created by discourse as much as discourse
is created by individual subjects in speech acts.

On one level discourse can be seen as a method of analysis that attributes
significance to language as the signifier of substantive entities. Fairclough
(1992) suggests that discourse can be seen as both textual analysis, in the sense
of the structure of language, and as specific to particular situations. Thus there
is 'marketing' discourse, 'counselling' discourse and perhaps even a 'housing'
discourse. The very use of a term, say 'problem estate', can help to 'create' the
entity itself.

Yet discourse theory goes further than merely an analysis of language and
becomes a thorough critique of ideology. As Torfing (1999) has suggested,
discourse is now used in a wider sense than mere texts and language. Following
Derrida (1978) and Laclau (1993), Torfing defines discourse as 'a decentred
structure in which meaning is constantly negotiated and constructed' (1999, p 40).
The structure is seen as 'an ensemble of signifying sequences' (p 40) and allows
for the inclusion of both physical and non-physical objects. This has allowed
housing researchers such as Jacobs et al (2003) and Ronald (2008) to contest the
ideological nature of owner occupation and, indeed, the RTB itself.

The article by Jacobs et al is particularly interesting because it directly uses the
example of the RTB. The authors suggest that discourse operates to legitimise a
particular policy strategy. This involves the identification of a social problem, for
which a particular policy mechanism to deal with it is then created. Discourse
is then used to legitimise this strategy. However, this discourse merely serves to
mask the fact that the policy prescription is actually determined to pursue a
narrow interest. Discourse, therefore, serves to align a sufficient body of opinion
to that interest. Accordingly, Jacobs et al are able to state that 'Policy is perhaps
best understood as operating within a contextual space in which competing actors
attempt to impose a version of reality concordant with their interests' (2003,
p 308). There are, therefore, various discourses which compete against each other
in a battle for dominance of the policy agenda.

In explaining the RTB, Jacobs et al argue for a '*discursive* shift' (2003, p 309)
in the policy of council house sales that went beyond the voluntary systems of
the 1970s. They argue that the Thatcher period saw an attempt to establish a
hegemonic position allowing for the development of owner occupation on a
more concerted basis. Hence the Conservatives developed a legitimising discourse
around certain notions, such as the fact that tenants were being 'exploited' by
municipal landlords, which itself was described as being 'feudal'. Tenants were
experiencing a form of oppression and 'serfdom' from which they needed to be
'liberated'. Jacobs et al pick out examples of this form of language in speeches
and policy documents from both local and national politicians from the mid- to

late 1970s. They conclude by suggesting that the RTB was a 'classic example of the successful mobilisation of bias' (2003, p 317).

This form of analysis based on looking at particular discourse has become increasingly popular in housing research since the 1980s. On the face of it, it offers an apparently sophisticated approach to housing analysis in that it shows that certain policies have become dominant. However, as I have discussed elsewhere (King, 2004b), this form of analysis does not actually explain anything, but merely describes it. As Somerville and Bengtsson (2002) have suggested, a key problem with the manner in which discourse is defined and deployed is that it excludes nothing. Everything is a form of discourse and so the theory can be applied in all circumstances. However, one purpose of a theory is to allow us to discriminate between concepts and arguments. Yet if everything is discourse, the theory is reducible to a catch-all banality and consequently allows for no real theoretical development.

Jacob et al's argument presumes some level of coordination between the various actors perpetrating the particular 'mobilisation of bias' that is the RTB. There is an assumption of some controlling mechanism where particular notions – serfdom, feudalism, exploitation – are coined and distributed: the particular interest has to have some means with which to coordinate its control. Yet this control mechanism remains hidden. The authors merely provide examples of the means of controlling, without explaining how it can be coordinated and so properly representative of a particular interest. The only means we can find in the article is hindsight, where the authors purport to find particular connections between phrases and words and assume that there is a therefore a formal association between them.

This notion of discourse analysis suffers from the same fault as its Marxist precursor, false consciousness. Both these notions cannot be falsified, but rather depend on an implicit assumption of circularity, whereby any argument seeking to denounce the identification of a particular discourse is seen as an example of that discourse at work. Those who wish to prosecute a particular interest quite naturally seek to destroy those arguments which lay that interest bare. Accordingly, notions of discourse cannot be gainsaid without making one's particular ideological interest clear.

This is not the place for a detailed discussion of the arguments for and against discourse theory and social constructionism,[2] but there is one general criticism that is particularly relevant to the discussion on the RTB. Both these theories can be seen as critiques of a purely objective reality. They do not question whether things exist or not, or whether there is a 'real world', but rather that reality is constructed by discourse. This means that reality – the state of things as they appear to be – is contingent and transformation is therefore possible. Both Hacking (1999) and Nozick (2001) argue that the appeal of social constructionism arises from a desire to transform society. If we insist that certain things are arbitrary and contingent we then have grounds for changing them. But is it not the case, argues Nozick, that what we see as social constructions are only those things we seek to change? Nozick suggests that referring to something as a social construction denudes that object of any authority, and thus it can (and therefore ought) to be changed. He suggests that social constructions are never 'good things' to be welcomed, but are things that the critic seeks to alter, change or improve. Thus, calling something a social construction gives one the grounds to challenge it. The need for more social housing is therefore never contested as a social construction, whilst owner occupation and the RTB are. The reason for this is that these particular theorists tend to support social housing and oppose the extension of owner occupation.

But why should this be? Why do the overwhelming majority of academics and commentators on housing issues see owner occupation as illegitimate and prefer social housing instead? If we can be somewhat perverse for a moment, we might wish to consider what particular interest there is in the 'mobilisation of bias' for social housing, even if we cannot claim it is a successful one. Accordingly, we might point to a professional interest in promoting state solutions for rented housing because of the particular nature of housing education and research in countries like the UK, which is largely sponsored by agencies which themselves fund, own and support social housing. Of course, this is to impugn the motives of particular researchers, which we do not particularly seek to do. Alternatively, of course, we might exonerate them by suggesting that researchers are themselves deluded by a particular ideological construct which has interests in promoting a certain form of state-based provision. But, we have no means of objectively verifying this outside of discourse theory itself, and so perhaps we are best to leave this line of argument here.

The final point we need to make is that defining the RTB as socially constructed out of a particular discourse may be an attempt to delegitimise it, but it does not make it go away. Referring to something as a social construction does not alter it (Nozick, 2001) or make its effects any less palpable. This again means we have to question what the point of referring to something as a social construction actually is. Is it just to make us feel better about certain things that we know already we do not like?

Just for the money

I want to turn now to a more practical series of arguments, namely those about money. It is not my intention to undertake a full discussion on the financial implications of the RTB, largely because, as with lots of issues relating to the RTB, it would largely be historical. The money is long gone and there is nothing we can do about it. Rather, I shall concentrate here on one of the most controversial issues: whether the RTB succeeded only because of the discounts offered, and whether these discounts could be justified.

We might argue that the success of the RTB was largely, if not solely, due to the discounts offered. The RTB allowed sitting tenants to buy their dwelling at a discount of a minimum of 32% and up to a maximum of 60%. Therefore, the real reason for the success of the RTB had nothing to do with a desire to own, but was, rather, due to financial inducements. In other words, 2.5 million households in the UK were effectively bribed to become owner-occupiers, and, therefore, most of these tenants would not have become owners without the RTB and the financial inducements it provided.

Clearly, the discounts helped in making the policy appear more appealing and doubtless caused many households to take up the offer. Yet, we should remember that many of these households had little or no experience of owner occupation. They were households who had never been owners, and did not come from a background where owning was the norm. These working-class households perhaps, therefore, needed some sort of incentivisation if they were to become owners as the Conservatives wished. These households, we might argue, needed to be eased into owner occupation.

This argument, of course, does not justify the use of discounts. The most common argument used is that tenants had paid rent for a number of years and the discounts were to account for this. However, in answer to this we could see rent payments as a user charge and so they relate only to the provision of the service of access to accommodation. Therefore rent payments are no different to buying a ticket for the cinema or hiring a car. In neither of these cases is there a suggestion that we deserve a discount because of these payments.

Rent charged bears no relation to the costs of production or current costs, but is, rather, set by a national policy. Rents are not based on actual costs but are set by government targets determined according to desired subsidy levels. Since 1996 central government has been effectively running local authority housing at a profit, in that rent contributions to Housing Benefit exceed government revenue subsidies (King, 2001). Moreover, rents are not related to the conditions of supply and demand. It is not a market or market-based rent, nor is there any necessary connection with the current costs of provision. Accordingly, a tenant living in an older house may have paid considerably more than the capital cost of the dwelling as well as the costs of management and maintenance.

But we also need to remember that social tenants have always received a subsidy. A majority of tenants receive Housing Benefit and those who pay their rent are doing so at below market levels. Therefore it is not the case that only RTB households were helped by the state. The average level of discount for England in 2006/07[3] was £24,970, which is a considerably lower percentage than in earlier years of the RTB (27%: see Table 4.3 in Chapter 4), but similar in money terms to past years. This, we should remember is a one-off subsidy and they receive no further state assistance.

However, council tenants have received considerable and ongoing subsidies. In 2006 the average weekly council rent in England was £57.69 compared with the average market rent in the private rented sector of £115.55. This means that council tenants were receiving an effective subsidy of £57.86 per week or an annual amount of £3,008.72 (Wilcox, 2008).

In addition, we need to remember that council tenants can effectively obtain a double subsidy. In 2006, 53% of council tenants were in receipt of Housing Benefit at an average of £51.70 per week or £2,688.40 per annum. Conceivably therefore, some council tenants might be in receipt of an effective subsidy of £5,697.12 per annum (Wilcox, 2008). Thus a council tenant might receive the same level of the RTB average discount in 4.3 years. This is particularly pertinent in that tenants must now be resident for five years to qualify for the RTB.

So current council tenants in receipt of Housing Benefit enjoy considerable levels of subsidy, which are easily comparable with those of RTB households. But these tenants can gain access to these subsidies with no qualifying period and without, of course, committing any of their own resources. Unlike RTB households, nothing is expected of Housing Benefit claimant households in return for their subsidies. We might argue that Housing Benefit households deserve their subsidies more than RTB households because of the situation in which they find themselves, but this presumes that these households have done nothing to precipitate their situation and that no alternatives are available to them.

What this suggests is that RTB households are not the only ones to be subsidised and that social tenants receive comparable amounts of subsidy and on terms that are less conditional. This implies that the subsidies to these households are not outlandish when we compare them with the current financial arrangements of social housing. This means that we have to return to the normative position of whether we see vulnerability – in the sense of being eligible for Housing Benefit – as outweighing consistency of behaviour and the need for a personal financial contribution.

Of course, there are many more financial issues we could consider and use to offset the arguments discussed here. We might seek to calculate issues like lost rent income, the fairness of capital gains to purchasers and so on. However, the point of this brief discussion has been to demonstrate that the financial issues are by no means clear-cut and that we can certainly make a financial case that justifies discounts in relation to subsidies offered to social tenants.

But this financial discussion does not necessarily justify the principles involved. Regardless of the relative position with social tenants, is it ever justified to offer subsidies to owner-occupiers? This is an interesting point because it shows that there are criticisms of the RTB from the right of the political spectrum.

Friendly fire?

We might presume that the RTB would be welcomed by all on the right. But this is to make a rather simplistic assumption about the homogeneity of the right.[4] Whilst many conservatives might see nothing particularly wrong with government intervention (depending on what the intervention involves), there is also a strong strand of classical liberal or libertarian thought in the so-called New Right (Green, 1987; King, 2006a). This particular strand of thought would question whether the government should intervene in housing markets, and whether subsidies to certain owner-occupiers might skew housing markets. Instead they would argue that the role of the government should be limited to maintaining low and stable interest rates and that is all. If social tenants wish to buy a house they are, of course, free to do so, but should not expect a subsidy from the government to assist them. Some libertarians might well accept that tenants should be able to buy their council dwelling, on the grounds that this frees them from state control, but again not at a discount.

In this regard the RTB is seen as a form of social engineering, which is viewed as illegitimate in that it seeks to manipulate the choices of individuals and alters their behaviour through the offering of incentives with the aim of meeting the specific aims of others. We might see that owner occupation is a good thing, but this should not be imposed on others through the use of incentives. It matters little that the aim of this particular form of social engineering is to create independence and personal responsibility.

This raises the more general issue of whether the state can act in order to make people free, or whether any decision must come from the individuals themselves (Narveson, 1988). We might see something of a tension here between liberty and responsibility. Indeed, the RTB shows the differences between the libertarian and conservative positions that were seen to be influential on the Conservative Party in the Thatcher period. First, the RTB encourages independence, personal responsibility, self-reliance and freedom from state interference. But, second, it only does so through the use of state power, from a government believing it knows what is best for its citizens. So the RTB relies on top-down direction and state subsidies targeted at specific deserving groups.

One way of dealing with this is to see the RTB not as social engineering, but simply as a form of privatisation. In this regard it merely returns housing to what might be called its 'natural' state of a market relation. The RTB, then, returns housing back to the situation it would have been prior to state intervention. We can quibble here about what is meant by natural – it might in this context be used in the Hayekian sense of arising not by intentional design but as a result of human interaction (Hayek, 1988) – but the point is that the RTB returns housing to the state it would have been in without state intervention.

However, regardless of the merits of this argument, we need to recognise that the RTB was primarily a conservative and not a libertarian policy. As I have argued in *A Conservative Consensus?* (King, 2006a), the RTB, like many policies of the Thatcher–Major period, showed the dominance of the practical and pragmatic response over the directly ideological. Whilst there is a clear ideological basis to the RTB, as we have seen in Chapter 3, what mattered to the Conservatives was that once they had decided upon a policy it should be made to work as well as possible. In Chapter 2 we discussed that conservatism is an ideology that is concerned rather more with process than outcome. This extrinsic sense is important for its connection to self-interest, personal responsibility and expectations, as well as a sense of what is practical and possible. All these notions are concerned with a sense of things on the surface, and, as we saw in Chapter 2, with keeping things close, and an immediacy of experience and response. Conservatism, unlike libertarianism and ideologies of the left, is dispositional and concerned with how individuals respond to incentives to create social stability. The RTB is a particular example of this conservative approach. This may disappoint libertarians, but the Conservatives would surely argue that the ends justify the means.

Perverse criticism

There is though now a different argument developing over the role of the government in supporting owner occupation, and this has arisen out of the collapse of housing markets as a result of the credit crunch of 2007/08. We can argue that this financial crisis has arisen because of government support to owner occupation and the desire that households have to own (Ferguson, 2008; Shiller, 2008). The sub-prime housing scandal in the US and the collapse of Northern Rock in the UK in 2007 have arisen out of the general encouragement of owner occupation by governments and their regulators.

This desire to own has also driven the RTB, and so we can question, in the light of what has happened since 2007, whether the government should support the desire to own and to use public resources to assist it. What we can ask, as several commentators and politicians have done, is what impact does the credit crunch and housing recession have on the RTB? Does it, and should it, alter our attitude towards the RTB in any fundamental way?

In December 2008, the National Housing Federation (NHF) called for the RTB to be suspended in the light of the housing crisis (Beattie, 2008). They argued that the increase in repossessions and lack of new building would increase the demand for social housing, and therefore it was not particularly appropriate to be selling social housing, which was already in short supply. Going somewhat further than the NHF, the Labour MP for Grimsby, Austin Mitchell, has called for the end of the RTB (Beattie, 2008). Mitchell is chair of the House of Commons' council housing group and argued that as private developers were going out of business, the only means of encouraging building was a drive for more council houses. Superficially we can see the appeal of this argument: that it is somehow immoral to be selling social housing at a discount precisely at a time when many households are struggling to maintain their mortgage and so keep their house.

However, a moment's reflection would show just how opportunistic such a call to suspend or end the RTB actually is. None of those dwellings sold in 2008, nor those that would be sold in 2009, would be empty and available for re-let. If the RTB was suspended we can safely assume that these tenants would not move out, as they would be unlikely to gain access to owner-occupied housing in any other way than through the RTB. The state of housing markets has cut off any alternative opportunities for this group as well as those with mortgage arrears. In addition, as we have seen in Chapter 4, one effect of the recession has been a collapse of RTB sales, which would mean that abolition would have little effect even if all the dwellings could be re-let. The NHF's statement was therefore either an example of muddled thinking, or an attempt to use the recession in housing markets to attack a policy which they have always been opposed to.

However, it was interesting that the government's response to the NHF was speedy and emphatic. They argued that the RTB was an essential part of their strategy for housing and so were opposed to any suspension. Equally interesting was the fact that there was little overt support for the NHF from other sources and so the story quickly died. No campaign was started against the RTB, which perhaps suggests that there was no appetite for tackling this issue, perhaps in the knowledge that the government would see abolition as politically suicidal, bringing back unfortunate memories of 1983 and Old Labour. Even though the RTB now only has a marginal effect, a nominally left-of-centre government still feels it has to openly support the policy.

But despite the government's continued support for the RTB, does it not look somewhat incongruous in a recession? It could be argued that any housing subsidy would be better spent on those in danger of losing their dwelling than on encouraging a change of tenure. But, again, an understanding of the nature of the RTB would show that this is just muddled thinking. In order to gain access to the subsidy provided to RTB households, social landlords would actually have to sell their dwellings. This is because the subsidy offered to RTB recipients is not a straightforward handout like a welfare benefit or grant, but takes the form of equity released from the value of the property on its sale. The subsidy remains trapped in the dwelling until an RTB application is made and goes through to sale.[5] Therefore the subsidy cannot be used for anything else unless the government sought to tax RTB households an amount equivalent to some or all of the value of their discount. Such a tax would only be workable at the point of resale and so would act as a form of permanent remittance. However, it is unlikely that any government could claim to support owner occupation at the same time as proposing such a tax.

What is particularly interesting about these recent arguments about the RTB is that the criticism has arisen not from a concern for social housing itself, but because of a collapse in owner occupation. Hence Austin Mitchell's argument for more council housing is based on the need to replace the dwellings not being built by private developers. The NHF argue that increasing repossessions and no new building will increase the demand for social housing. But neither of these arguments is based on a clear and principled support for social housing. Rather they seem to rely on the normality of owner occupation as the majority tenure and the possibility of social housing helping to support it in a crisis. There is an implicit assumption here of the central role of owner occupation and that social housing can only be justified as a tenure subsidiary to it. There is almost a wilful perversity in these arguments which call for the ending of a policy which encourages owner occupation because social housing is needed to support owner-occupiers.

We might argue that criticisms of the RTB are somewhat beside the point after such a decline in 2008. However, what this discussion has shown is a change in the nature of the criticism. Instead of a concern for social housing, what seems to matter now is the state of housing markets and what role other tenures might play in supporting it. Thus we might suggest that we live in a post–RTB world, where the arguments we hear against the RTB derive from a concern, sincere or otherwise, for the state of owner occupation. It may be that this is purely opportunistic and these critics have always been opposed to the RTB. But regardless of this it tells us that the nature of the debate regarding the RTB has changed quite fundamentally. We can suggest that this change is actually due, in part at least, to the effect of the RTB in encouraging owner occupation.

Of course, we can expect the criticisms of the RTB to be sustained, simply because there are those who seek to promote the interest of social housing. These criticisms will continue to range from the crude and opportunistic to the theoretically sophisticated. But there is no reason to suggest that these criticisms will become more successful. All the main political parties maintain a clear support for owner occupation, and the RTB has a symbolic significance in demonstrating this support and the recession has made this even clearer. The question that remains is whether this makes the RTB unique: is the success of the RTB just down to good luck and a happy coming together of interests and circumstance, or is there something more general we can learn for policy making? This is the question to which we now turn.

Notes

[1] I have had several discussions with academics and housing professionals who have assured me that stock transfer under Labour was different from the Conservative version. This apparently was because Labour consulted before imposing it, whilst the Tories just imposed it.

[2] See King (2004b) for a detailed critique.

[3] I have taken this year as this is the last complete set of RTB and rent data available at the time of writing.

[4] Again I am grateful to the regular contributors to the IEA's blog for their comments on the RTB and its legitimacy.

[5] Actually, we might argue that the subsidy only becomes realised if and when the dwelling is sold on by the RTB household.

SIX

What does it tell us?

Introduction

We might see that after 30 years the Right to Buy (RTB) is left in a rather strange position. On the one hand, it has clearly had a transformative effect on housing in the UK. It has created 2.5 million new owner-occupiers and helped to contract social housing to a fraction of its former size and influence. It has been the source of more vitriol and ideologically charged controversy than any other housing policy. But, on the other hand, by 2008 it had shrunk to a tiny trickle of sales compared to the early 1980s, and because of the nature of current social housing tenants, this is unlikely to change dramatically even if economic circumstances were to become more favourable.

This might suggest that much of the importance of the RTB is historical. It was an interesting episode in the history of housing policy and one that caused much controversy and debate, but which is now over and we can move on. But this presumes that there is nothing left to learn about the policy. Surely we need to understand why it worked so well, and whether this can be replicated in policies in the future? Why has no other housing policy, and public policy more generally, been anything like so transformative? Was it just luck on the part of the Conservatives in 1979 that they found the right set of circumstances, or is there something more significant in the policy?

These are the questions that we shall consider in this chapter. We have now a full understanding of the intellectual underpinnings of the policy, what it sought to achieve, what it did and what impact it had. We have looked at arguments in favour of the policy and those against it. So we can now assess what the RTB meant and why it had the impact it did. Are there some principles that we can extract from the RTB that can inform policy making, or is it a case of a government getting lucky and then claiming it really meant it all along? Of course, if the RTB is a one-off this will alter how we look at it and what we can learn from it. But perhaps there might still be some lessons, even if they are less significant.

So what we shall do here is to try to get to the essence of the RTB, both in general and specific terms, to assess why it worked and whether there is anything we can learn from this that informs policy making. This does not mean that we will be able to create a template that we can then readily apply to other circumstances. But what we can develop is some sense of why the RTB worked and what combination of circumstances, interests and resources need to come together for policy to be effective.

This debate, needless to say, depends on what sorts of policy we see as useful and effective. Public policy can be used to direct or to facilitate, to control or to empower, to manipulate or to withdraw. Different people, because of their politics and interests, will seek quite different things from policy, and we must assume good faith and fine intentions in all cases. What this means is that the principles that we derive out of the RTB might appear to be as uncongenial to some as the RTB itself. This is, of course, fair enough. But what we all need to recognise is that the RTB was an uncommon policy: uncommon in terms of its impact and its consequences. This ought to mean that we have something significant to learn and this should be recognised even by those who fundamentally disagree with what the RTB sought to achieve. Having said this, any principles that are derived from the RTB will likely be tainted, if that is the right word, with the same spirit. But, then, this might just be a significant point too.

We begin the discussion in this chapter by looking at whether the RTB was just a matter of lucky circumstance, or whether we can see it as an example of forward planning and clear thinking. Having done this we make some brief comments on what the history of the RTB tells us about social housing. Next, the chapter considers why the policy worked and what we can learn from it in terms of general policy making and issues specific to housing. This leads to a consideration of what is the essence of the RTB: its direct link to the manner in which we use our housing. The chapter ends with a statement of some core principles that I see as fundamental to the RTB.

Just lucky?

Politicians like to suggest that what they do is well planned and thought through, and there is certainly some evidence this was the case with the RTB. However, it still might have been merely a combination of happy circumstances that allowed for the great success of the RTB. There were a large number of suitable households, with the income and opportunity to take advantage of the offer. The right incentives, both financial and material, were presented, with 6 million dwellings available. The Conservatives could implement the policy as soon as parliament and practicality allowed, and it had no immediate cost to government. Unlike other policies, it did not involve any subsidy or upfront funding. In fact, the government benefited from reduced borrowing and returned capital receipts. The RTB can be said to have caught the imagination of people by being simple and straightforward to comprehend. It was obvious what the policy was about and it did not need much selling or explaining: the benefits to individual households were obvious.

It may well be that this particular combination of circumstances cannot be repeated, and so we might see the RTB's success as mere luck. It was where a combination of circumstances just happened to come together. However, we might be more charitable and suggest that it took a considerable degree of awareness to realise the potential that could be made from these circumstances.

One of the problems in housing policy, particularly post-1987, has been that governments have sought vainly for the next big idea to compete with the RTB. Successive governments seem to have been searching for the magical policy that transforms housing just like the RTB. Policies such as Tenants' Choice, Housing Action Trusts (DOE, 1987) and Sustainable Communities (ODPM, 2003) have all been trumpeted as policies that would transform housing. But it might well be that there is no other policy where such a peculiar confluence of circumstance, imaginative design and cultural relevance all come together. Such success cannot be planned for in advance.

However, as we discussed in some detail in Chapter 3, the RTB was certainly intended. The Conservatives believed that many households desired to buy and constructed a scheme that allowed them to do so using existing resources. The dwellings were not built between 1920 and 1980 so that they could be sold, but clearly their existence mattered. Likewise, without design, there were a large number of current council tenants willing and able to take up the opportunity of the RTB. And, of course, the whole idea of the RTB only made sense if there were council houses with tenants living in them.

What we should conclude, therefore, is that the RTB was part planning and part circumstance. But this is really no different than many other policies, which start from current circumstances and resources. The difference with the RTB compared with policies such as Tenants' Choice is that the thinking behind it was based on something significant (King, 2006b). Successful politics, we might say, is the proper and acute recognition of circumstance. This being so, we can look at some lessons that we might learn from the RTB.

What does it mean for social housing?

One key lesson of the RTB is that central government, if it wishes to, can use social housing with virtual impunity. No government will lose popularity as a result of attacking social housing and using its resources to benefit other sectors. Indeed, it might even gain popularity, especially if the policy is to turn social housing into owner occupation. There is no political constituency for social housing, but a huge one for owner occupation. The RTB, of course, has exacerbated this, in that over 2.5 million council dwellings were transferred into the owner-occupied sector. But this situation was clearly evident in 1979 in that there was no effective opposition to the RTB.

This shows the relative political and electoral weightings that exist between owning and renting. This is partly because of the relative size of the two tenures, but there are also other factors which we need to take into account. First, there is the importance of the distinction between means-tested services such as social housing and more universal ones such as education and health care (King, 2003; 2009). Universal services, which all households have ready access to, tend to be more popular and, therefore, to have greater electoral significance. Successive governments have increased funding to health and education whilst cutting spending on social housing. The privatisation of health care is hugely controversial, whilst the privatisation of council housing has happened and is generally seen as electorally popular.

Second, and this is a point we shall discuss in more detail later, the government's attitude towards social housing shows that it has understood the significance of the private over the social when it comes to housing. Policies such as the RTB recognise the manner in which we experience housing: as households within private space. We do not experience housing socially or collectively, but as individuals living in households. The RTB played on this sense by transferring control of the dwelling directly over to the household and away from a landlord purportedly acting in the collective interest.

So successive governments have felt able to use social housing for wider purposes and take political credit for doing so. The question remains, however, whether this is just something particular to social housing, or whether we can take some general lessons from it.

Why it worked

Housing has an inbuilt advantage in terms of public policy reform (King, 2003; 2009). It is more amenable to private provision than is the case with health and education. This is because housing need is permanent and predictable. We always need housing and our needs do not normally change rapidly, unlike the unpredictability of our need for health care. Even the needs of homeless households are easy to establish and remain stable. What matters, of course, is the capability of the individual household to fulfil their need (King, 2003). As a result of this predictability we are more able to understand our housing need and plan accordingly. This means that housing is more open to market-based provision. We can argue, then, that housing was always more likely to be a target for privatisation than other welfare services.

But this of itself does not explain the transformative effect of the RTB. As we have seen, governments since 1987 have sought in vain for a big idea to follow on from the RTB. So what was it about the RTB that made it such a success? On the basis of our discussion in this book we can point to a number of sound reasons why the RTB worked so well. Some of these are quite specific to the policy, but others are more readily transferable.

The first point is that the RTB had very clear aims. It was easy to understand what the policy was for and it was all too clear what its benefits were. It genuinely worked to the advantage of individuals and this was obviously apparent. A second crucial factor is that the policy was not quickly repealed and so could settle down. Indeed, the policy quickly took hold and had the effect desired of it. The RTB had an impetus and quite quickly became a part of the normal environment in which housing policy operates. It became clear after the 1983 General Election that it had considerable political support and was not going away. Third, it was equally important that the policy was well targeted on a group that was large enough to matter. There were a large number of working council tenants who had sufficient money to buy, but who were already settled in a dwelling that they knew intimately and enjoyed. These households had a reasonable and permanent income to support their aspiration to be owners. This gave the RTB an advantage over other policies such as Homebuy or shared ownership, which are partial, give people only a limited choice and are for people who by definition have insufficient money to buy on the open market. Fourth, we have to say that it was something which very many tenants wanted.

Fifth, as a policy the RTB was readily containable, in that it related to a specific set of dwellings and households. It had only a few variables which could be managed comfortably by the government. In addition, any opposition to the policy could be readily managed by regulation and incentives (Malpass and Murie, 1999; Sillars, 2007). In other words, it was possible for the government to retain its control over the policy and ensure that it operated to the advantage of tenants and itself. This was a policy that could not be readily captured by professionals or other interests.

Sixth, the RTB was a genuinely proactive policy, in that it could be planned out and therefore started from scratch. It did not arise from a reaction to events, from a particular problem or crisis. The government was able to establish the policy on its terms and in its own time and so it could be set up with some certainty.

The factors discussed so far are all somewhat general and do not necessarily relate to the specifics of buying and selling council housing. There are, however, a number of more specific reasons why the RTB worked so well and why it can be seen as a model for other areas of public policy. An important issue is that the RTB plays on the personal rather than the public. It relies on self-interest and not an abstract altruism. It connects with the actual expectations and aspirations that individuals have to own their own dwelling, rather than vague notions like solidarity, where we are expected to have strong feelings towards anonymous others. Furthermore, the RTB encourages personal control over resources which allows households the certainty to plan ahead and use their assets as they see fit, and this control is permanent and continuous. It is not means tested or contingent on circumstances. The RTB, therefore, creates a real and permanent change for the household. This change would be politically and financial expensive to undo, which again allows for certainty and consistency in household decision making.

The RTB is important because it fundamentally and permanently alters the relationship between individuals and the state. It limits future government intervention in the household. Households are no longer beholden to bureaucratic intervention and to decisions taken by others according to priorities other than those of the household. The RTB offers a subsidy, but this is limited to the initial discount and then there is no more access to subsidy. The subsidy had no immediate effect on government spending or the tax burden of individuals. Indeed, it might be said to have lightened the government's burden in time through a reduction in public debt. So the RTB has the distinct virtue that the liability to the tax-payer is limited and not open-ended as is the case with Housing Benefit. Indeed, purchasing the dwelling cuts the household off from access to other subsidies such as Housing Benefit.

The RTB forces people to take care of themselves and their loved ones and this responsibility cannot easily be pushed back onto the state. As Schmidtz (1998) has argued, public policy should seek to internalise responsibility rather than forcing people to rely on external agents like the state. Schmidtz states that responsibility 'is internalised when agents take responsibility: for their welfare, for their futures, for the consequences of their actions' (p 8). He suggests that 'property rights are pre-eminent among institutions that lead people to take responsibility for their welfare' (p 22). He goes so far as to suggest that 'institutions of property [are] the human race's most pervasive and most successful experiment in internalised responsibility' (p 25). What internalises responsibility more effectively than anything else is the attribution of property rights to individuals.

More controversially perhaps, we can suggest that the RTB allows for housing assets to be recycled and for this to have an effect on the wider economy. Council housing, we might suggest, is something of a dead asset in that it cannot be used for borrowing purposes and it is therefore equity which cannot be accessed. The RTB allows for this equity to be released into the wider economy. It brings the dwelling and the household into the mainstream housing tenure, rather than keeping them isolated in a residualised tenure.

Some of the factors we have considered here are indeed circumstantial. The RTB needed there to be a stock of dwellings and a number of willing participants. Yet, it is also clear that it was more than circumstance that created the success of the RTB. The policy created permanent and irreversible change that materially benefited the participants. This was because it played on private interests in a clear and readily understandable manner. What mattered in particular was that households were able to use their dwelling in a different manner as a result of the policy.

Private use

As we have stated, what really matters with the RTB is the changed relationship between household and dwelling. No longer is the household beholden to the council for repairs or under its control in terms of how residents can use or change their dwelling. The household is now tasked with this, which some might find onerous, and others might relish, but all have taken on by choice. Households can now do with the dwelling what they want to, change doors and windows and make it look how they think it should. Alternatively they can choose to leave it exactly as it is. Whichever route is taken, they can do things on their own terms and in their own way. Like all owners, their relationship is with their mortgage lender and not any more complicated than that. It is impersonal and distant and entirely formal. Households have entered the realm of really private finance, where their affairs are no longer settled by public policy. Of course, the household remains in the same dwelling which retains whatever facilities and qualities it had prior to its purchase. However, the use the household now has is extended to include the right to alter, to develop and even to dispose. The household's rights are more extensive, and the rights of the 'public' are diminished accordingly.

This clear legal change might also have psychological implications in terms of how the dwelling is perceived. It is now almost certainly the most valuable asset the household has, and one that, in more years than not, will appreciate in value and so we might think that it will increase in importance. This will create a sense of financial security to add to the physical and psychological security of the dwelling.

The sense of *mineness* – that the dwelling belongs to us in an emotional as well as legal sense – is important even as it might remain inchoate and unformed (King, 2008). The dwelling, before purchase, may have been a place of birth, nurture and development, and so fulfil the need for emotional and ontological security (King, 1996). Yet this is only added to by ownership (Saunders, 1990). We should not fall into the trap of making a necessary connection between ownership and ontological or emotional security, but should rather see ownership as additive. We might suggest that ownership contributes an extra layer that confirms the security, and develops it through an enhanced sense of use.

We might suggest that it is the *sense* of use that changes, but not the use itself. We sense the dwelling differently and feel we relate to it in a more thorough and complex way. Part of this is the sense that we have chosen the dwelling rather than had it allocated to us. We are there, and can remain there, because of our actions and not because of criteria set by others. We may be aware that the choice is not perfect and, if money and supply conditions allowed, we might choose something altogether different. But within these constraints, we are there because we choose to be and stay there because of what it still fulfils. Our sense of what the dwelling means to us is therefore enhanced. Undoubtedly, this sense of use can turn sour, and the dwelling can become a handicap, if we find we cannot use it as we wish, if we cannot sustain the sort of life we want, or if we can no longer afford the dwelling. But even this latter feeling derives from this changed sense, this heightened *closeness* with the dwelling that comes from the fact that it is ours and not someone else's. We are there because we can and choose to be, we are not beholden to others; it is not conditional on anything but our income and our aspirations. The conditionality, as it were, is self-constructed and not made by others such as a landlord.

We can argue whether this makes owning better, and for many it will appear as if it does. There is really little doubt that owning is vastly more popular than renting. But what really matters is the sense of heightening which derives from the enhanced use. What is important, therefore, is that people perceive that their situation – where they are now at, what they are now experiencing – is better for them. We cannot properly gainsay this with dry academic arguments about the hidden costs of owning, or call what owners have a 'myth'. We can only acknowledge a sense of difference that permeates the use of dwelling through ownership.

The proof of this changed sense – if proof is the correct concept here – is that most households do not actually own the dwelling but are, of course, paying off a long-term loan to cover the cost of the dwelling. It may well be that our sense of the dwelling changes again once we have paid off our mortgage, but most people act as if they own it, and, equally important, they are treated as if they do.

An ex-council house is the same as it was when it was owned by the council. It may be adjoined to dwellings still owned by the council and the household may still see council workers (or more likely private contractors) cutting the grass in the communal areas. It may still look the same as their neighbours' and so those looking at it may assume it is still council owned (or, perhaps, council housing now being quite rare, they might now assume that all the households are owner-occupiers). Yet to those who now own it and use it, it will appear different, separate and special. This sense of the special is perhaps only felt by them, but they are all that matter. Just like any owner, we are the only ones *inside* and so only we can see it how it is, know that what it does is special to us. Only we can use it, only we can say that it is *ours* and know that is not conditional on the actions of others.

This is the outcome of the desire to own; it is where it is fulfilled. The virtue of the RTB – why it worked – is that it transformed this desire into actuality, into this heightened sense of use that comes from control. The RTB, in all its practicality of discounts and qualifying periods, and with all the controversy that surrounds it, fulfilled the desire to own for millions of people who would otherwise have been denied it. Very few policies can claim anything like such a result.

Some principles

So to conclude this discussion, we can state a number of principles that are crucial to the success of the RTB, and which might be extended to other policies. This is not intended as the basis for all successful policies, but rather shows the specific genius of the RTB. This is why, we might say, it worked.

First, the RTB sought to free up individuals rather than to burden them. It was genuinely aspirational rather than being based on social or collectivist notions of what individuals ought to do for anonymous others. There was, therefore, nothing abstract about the relations it created.

Second, it assumed that individuals were capable of looking after themselves, and that they could and would take responsibility for themselves and those around them. The RTB internalised responsibility and did not leave it to others.

Third, the RTB was based on how people actually are, rather than how politicians and ideologues of left or right might wish them to be. It was not based on a perfectionist view of human nature, but a conservative view of the world where it was understood that individuals seek to maintain things close to them.

We can use these principles for the assessment of policy and for the generation of new policy. These principles are general, but what they tell us is that we need to trust the capability of individuals and genuinely transfer control over to them.

The basis of public policy should be to empower and enable rather than merely provide services for people based on some abstract standard. Furthermore, we should not make assumptions about what people might want, or base this on some particular abstraction of human nature. Rather we should attempt to understand the aspirations that individuals have and seek to fulfil them. This sounds simple, but as we can see from most other housing policies since 1980, it is actually hard to achieve. There is a tendency to project a particular vision onto policy making that suits our prejudices, and the result is that we fail to achieve policies that work.

SEVEN

Conclusions

On the one hand, there is now little more to say. This book has sought to understand the Right to Buy (RTB) and explain its impact. It has been a book that has deliberately distinguished itself from the mainstream of writing on the RTB by concentrating not on criticising the policy but rather on explaining it. The result has been, for the most part, a fairly narrow focus, but this has allowed the RTB to stand up on its own. On the other hand, this approach has meant that there has been a lot left out. This is the price paid for trying to be different. But with the large existing literature there seems little point in trying to be comprehensive and include all the various arguments, especially as this would tend to water down the argument that I wished to present. So I stand by the approach taken in this book and what I wish to do here is merely reiterate some of the key points.

The first point is to state again that we need to view the RTB as a self-contained entity. Of course, the policy had wide-ranging effects and impacted considerably on other tenures. But it is only through this narrow focus that we can properly understand the RTB and get beyond the misunderstandings of the RTB that permeate the literature. In particular, we need to consider what the Conservatives intended with the RTB and how it fitted into their world view. It is not sufficient just to see the RTB in terms of its impact on other tenures. If we do this we will never appreciate why it worked and, by implication, why many other policies have failed.

Second, we need to reiterate just what an impact the RTB actually did have. The policy created over 2.5 million new owner-occupiers. This makes it hugely significant compared with most, if not all, other housing policies. No other policy can claim to have had such an effect with the exception of the building of council housing itself. Many housing policies are short-lived and limited in their scope. Some, such as Tenants' Choice and Housing Actions Trusts, fail completely (King, 1996) and others are only implemented after being watered down to the extent of being virtually useless, as in the case of Home Information Packs (King, 2009). We need to understand why the RTB could have such an impact, whilst other policies, equally well resourced and promoted, fail.

Third, the RTB was one of the most explicitly ideological of policies, both in terms of its promotion of owner occupation and the running down of social housing. But, we can also say that the response to the RTB has also been intensely ideological. The RTB, particularly in the early 1980s, provided a key ideological fault line. This ideological response is still very prevalent in the academic and policy literature on the RTB, as we have seen in Chapter 5. But having said this, we need to realise that the Conservatives were sufficiently pragmatic to make it work through offering discounts and where necessary reducing the qualifying periods.

But we have also seen that many local authorities now seem to depend on the RTB for a steady source of funding, and so its decline in 2008 has caused them difficulties. What this shows is that housing systems adapt and evolve. Policies that are initially opposed and even vilified, in time become part of the system and are then taken for granted and relied upon. This makes them hard to change or abolish without considerable disruption and spill-over effects. Housing systems are open and dynamic, which means that they are influenced in unpredictable ways, and issues and policies can interact in ways that are unforeseen. This means that it is difficult to attribute cause and effect and so state categorically what impact particular policies have had. Therefore we cannot completely extricate the impact of the RTB, even if we are able to isolate the aims and intentions behind the policy.

The fact that the RTB is in decline is important too. It might be that the credit crunch effectively kills it off, or it might make a comeback if and when housing markets return to some sense of normality. But the constraints placed on the RTB since 1999 have had their impact, as has the changed demography of social housing. Most tenants are not in work and so do not have the income to purchase their property, even if they do qualify. But an increasing number of tenants are now outside the scheme as a result of stock transfer. It is therefore very unlikely that we shall return to the large number of sales we saw in the 1980s and early 1990s.

But does it matter that it has declined? The policy has by now had much of its impact and this cannot practically be undone. The 2.5 million dwellings will not be returned to social landlords: they will never have the resources to fund this, never mind the political will. The RTB, we can surmise, can be maintained in its present form to deal with what demand there may be. What we should avoid, however, are any attempts to force more council sales regardless of circumstances. Proposals such as equity sharing and allowing tenants to use Housing Benefit payments to build up equity are fraught with dangers for tenants and landlords alike and are of such administrative and legal complexity that they are better avoided. The virtue of the RTB was its straightforwardness and simplicity. It also worked because many households had the wherewithal to participate. This situation cannot be artificially induced without risk, particularly for tenants.

This takes us to the question of whether anything can ever match up to the RTB. It is indeed difficult to see anything comparable in housing, as we have seen with several policies since the later 1980s which have sought to recreate the great success of the RTB. Beyond housing, we might point to a number of possibilities such as charter schools, offering parents the right to set up and manage new schools, or co-payments in health care which would allow for the development of a private insurance market to cover part payments. But we can only speculate on whether the right combination of aspirations, resources and political will can be mustered to back up either of these, even if they do seem to share the same principles as the RTB.

The big imponderable, as we near the end of the first decade of the third millennium, is the state of housing markets. Is the downturn that began in 2007 merely a temporary blip like those in the 1970s, 1980s and 1990s? If so, we can expect house prices to rise again and markets to normalise. But if this recession proves to be different and leads to considerable changes in the financial sector, we might be looking at a changed set of circumstances where the culture of support for owner occupation begins to shift. The popularity of owner occupation was not an overnight occurrence, but has taken generations to develop, helped by government policy and rising affluence. This means that expectations will only change slowly and perhaps only if we experience a truly cataclysmic crisis. Were this to happen, we might see the desire to own dissipate.

But this begs the question of what would replace owner occupation. Falling support for owner occupation would not necessarily lead to an increase in support for social housing. Why should our views about owner occupation necessarily dispose us towards a tenure we know to be residualised and unpopular? Moreover, why would a collapse in housing markets increase our knowledge of social housing and our preparedness to accept renting when we have been brought up to expect to own? In this regard, we need to reiterate that the RTB was a policy based on a perception that many desired to own. The Conservatives believed that many council tenants yearned for the opportunity to own their own dwelling. The RTB was in this sense not speculative or opportunistic, but based on an intelligent idea of what many households wanted. As we have seen in Chapter 3, this idea was in turn based on a coherent philosophy. What this shows is that many, perhaps a majority of, council tenants, who knew what renting from the local authority was all about, still preferred owner occupation. Why, then, should we expect those with no direct experience of social housing to suddenly change their perceptions. It may be that this comes about because of some as yet unforeseen disaster. But this would still mean that social housing was the last resort and not the tenure of choice.

So where does this leave us? Perhaps we can say that the best days of the RTB are behind it, and that its continuation will be more symbolic than actual. But its continual existence shows that owner occupation remains the priority and that there is nothing that can supplant it.

We should see the RTB as a relatively rare example of a policy that accords with human nature. It goes with the grain of human expectations and aspirations, whilst also working clearly and obviously for the benefit of government too. It made millions of people's lives better, and thoroughly altered their prospects and possibilities. In this sense it can be seen as a key example of the government acting positively, competently and benignly. If we wanted an example of how the government can intervene to improve the lives of millions of people, then the RTB is perhaps the best recent example. It shows the government working for the material benefit of its citizens by the creative use of public assets. It ought, therefore, to be seen as a key example by supporters of government intervention, as a policy that is clearly more effective than any other policy before or since. It achieved what the government intended with a relatively small administrative burden and little in the way of direct costs to the government, but with a huge impact on the lives of millions of people.

Why then is it so derided, particularly by those who purport to support the interests of working-class households? Perhaps we should see a similarity here to the way that many feminists viewed Mrs Thatcher as the first woman Prime Minister in Britain (Berlinski, 2008). Instead of seeing this as a huge positive and worthy of rejoicing, Mrs Thatcher was derided as a 'man in a dress', or as the 'wrong sort of woman'. Being a right-wing Tory she somehow did not count as a role model for feminists.

Likewise, the RTB has been seen as the 'wrong' sort of government intervention. It helped people in the 'wrong' way, or helped the 'wrong' sort of people. The RTB did not target the vulnerable, but rather was universal in its scope, offering the right to anyone who was a tenant for more than two years. It was 'wrong' because it involved the selling off of public assets bought with tax- and rate-payers' money. It was considered a problem in that it might embourgeois working-class households, filling them with a false consciousness that they were now part of the property-owning capitalist class (Honderich, 1990). And, of course, the RTB attacked what was seen as the main manifestation of municipal socialism. Perhaps what upset people was the temerity of the Conservatives in presuming that they knew what working-class people wanted. Or perhaps it was the fact that the Conservatives were so clearly correct in their presumptions.

For those on the right, who are generally suspicious of government intervention, this derision of the RTB is both immensely ironic and hugely amusing. Here we have a situation of massive government intervention in housing, but with the explicit aim of liberating households from the influence of the state. The RTB shows that government action can work, but, ironically, it is not a policy that the supporters of state intervention seem able to take to heart. Perhaps something better will come along one day.

Bibliography

Adams, I. (1993) *Political Ideology Today*, Manchester: Manchester University Press.

Althusser, L. (1968) *Reading Capitalism*, London: New Left Books.

Balchin, P. (1995) *Housing Policy: An Introduction*, 3rd edn, London: Routledge.

Beattie, J. (2008) 'Maggie Thatcher's council house scheme must go say MPs', *Daily Mirror*, 29 November 2008, accessed on 15 March 2009 at: http://www.mirror.co.uk/news/top-stories/2008/11/29/maggie-thatcher-s-council-house-scheme-must-go-say-mps-115875-20933805/

Berlinski, C. (2008) *There is No Alternative: Why Margaret Thatcher Matters*, New York: Basic Books.

Boyson, R. (1978) *Centre Forward: A Radical Conservative Programme*, London: Temple Smith.

Brown, T. and King, P. (2005) 'The power to choose: Effective choice and housing policy', *European Journal of Housing Policy*, vol 5, no 1, pp 59–75.

Burke, E. (1999) *Select Works, Volume 2: Reflections on the Revolution in France*, Indianapolis: Liberty Fund.

Butler, E. (2009) 'The financial crisis: Blame governments, not bankers', in P. Booth (ed) *Verdict on the Crash: Causes and Policy Implications*, London: Institute of Economic Affairs, pp 51–8.

Castells, M. (1977) *The Urban Question: A Marxist Appraisal*, London: Matthew Arnold.

CLG (Communities and Local Government) (2007) *Homes for the Future: More Affordable, More Sustainable*, London: The Stationery Office.

Conservative Party (1976) *The Right Approach*, London: Conservative Party, accessed on 3 March 2009 at: http://www.margaretthatcher.org/archive/displaydocument.asp?docid=109439

Conservative Party (1979) *Conservative General Election Manifesto 1979*, London: Conservative Party, accessed on 3 March 2009 at: http://www.margaretthatcher.org/archive/displaydocument.asp?docid=110858

Coulter, A. (1998) *High Crimes and Misdemeanors: The Case Against Bill Clinton*, Washington: Regnery Press.

Coulter, A. (2005) *Treason: Liberal Treachery from the Cold War to the War on Terror*, New York: Random House.

Derrida, J. (1978) *Writing and Difference*, London: Routledge.

DETR (Department of the Environment, Transport and the Regions) (2000) *Quality and Choice: A Decent Home for All*, London: DETR/DSS.

Devigne, R. (1994) *Recasting Conservatism: Oakeshott, Strauss, and the Response to Postmodernism*, New Haven: Yale University Press.

DoE (Department of the Environment) (1987) *Housing: The Government's Proposals*, London: HMSO.

DoE (1995) *Our Future Homes: Opportunity, Choice and Responsibility*, London: HMSO.

DWP (Department for Work and Pensions) (2002) *Building Choice and Responsibility: A Radical Agenda for Housing Benefit*, London: DWP.

Fairclough, N. (1992) *Discourse and Social Change*, Cambridge: Polity.

Ferguson, N. (2008) *The Ascent of Money: A Financial History of the World*, London: Allen Lane.

Field, F. (1976) *De We Need Council Houses?*, Occasional paper no 2, London: Catholic Aid Society.

Giddens, A. (1994) *Beyond Left and Right: The Future of Radical Politics*, Cambridge: Polity.

Gottfried, P. (1986) *The Search for Historical Meaning: Hegel and the Postwar American Right*, Dekalb, IL: Northern Illinois University Press.

Gramsci, A. (1971) *Selections from the Prison Notebooks*, London: Lawrence and Wishart.

Green, D. (1987) *The New Right: The Counter-Revolution in Political, Economic and Social Thought*, London: Harvester-Wheatsheaf.

Green, E. (2006) *Thatcher*, London: Hodder Arnold.

Hacking, I. (1999) *The Social Construction of What?*, Cambridge, MA: Harvard University Press.

Hayek, F. (1960) *The Constitution of Liberty*, London: Routledge.

Hayek, F. (1978) *New Studies in Philosophy, Politics, Economics and the History of Ideas*, London: Routledge.

Hayek, F. (1988) *The Fatal Conceit: The Errors of Socialism*, London: Routledge.

Hegel, G. (1991) *Elements of the Philosophy of Right*, Cambridge: Cambridge University Press.

Heidegger, M. (1962) *Being and Time*, Oxford: Blackwell.

Heseltine, M. (1978) *The Sale of Council Houses*, accessed on 3 March 2009 at: http://www.margaretthatcher.org/archive/displaydocument.asp?docid=110269

Hills, J. (2007) *Ends and Means: The Future Roles of Social Housing in England*, London: London School of Economics.

Honderich, T. (1990) *Conservatism*, London: Hamish Hamilton.

Jacobs, K., Kemeny, J. and Manzi, T. (2003) 'Privileged or exploited council tenants? The discursive change in Conservative housing policy from 1972–1980', *Policy & Politics*, vol 31, no 3, pp 307–20.

Jenkins, S. (1995) *Accountable to None: The Tory Nationalisation of Britain*, London: Hamish Hamilton.

Jones, C. and Murie, M. (2006) *The Right to Buy: Analysis and Evaluation of a Housing Policy*, Oxford: Blackwell.

Kekes, J. (1998) *A Case for Conservatism*, Ithaca, NY: Cornell University Press.

Kemeny, J. (1981) *The Myth of Home Ownership: Public Versus Private Choices in Housing Tenure*, London: Routledge.

Kemeny, J. (2005) '"The really big trade-off" between home ownership and welfare: Castles' evaluation of the 1980 thesis, and a reformulation 25 years on', *Housing Theory and Society*, vol 22, no 2, pp 59–75.

King, P. (1996) *The Limits of Housing Policy: A Philosophical Investigation*, London: Middlesex University Press.

King, P. (2000) 'Individuals and competence', in P. King and M. Oxley (eds) *Housing: Who Decides?*, Basingstoke: Macmillan, pp 9–69.

King, P. (2001) *Understanding Housing Finance*, London: Routledge.

King, P. (2003) *A Social Philosophy of Housing*, Aldershot: Ashgate.

King, P. (2004a) *Private Dwelling: Contemplating the Use of Housing*, London: Routledge.

King, P. (2004b) 'Relativism, subjectivity and the self: A critique of social constructionism', in K. Jacobs, J. Kemeny and T. Manzi (eds) *Social Constructionist Methods and their Application to Housing Studies*, Aldershot: Ashgate.

King, P. (2005) *The Common Place: The Ordinary Experience of Housing*, Aldershot: Ashgate.

King, P. (2006a) *A Conservative Consensus? Housing Policy Before 1997 and After*, Exeter: Imprint Academic.

King, P. (2006b) *Choice and the End of Social Housing*, London: Institute of Economic Affairs.

King, P. (2008) *In Dwelling: Implacability, Exclusion and Acceptance*, Aldershot: Ashgate.

King, P. (2009) *Understanding Housing Finance: Meeting Needs and Making Choices*, 2nd edn, London: Routledge.

Kirk, R. (1985) *The Conservative Mind: From Burke to Eliot*, 7th revised edn, Washington, DC: Regnery Press.

Klein, N. (2007) *The Shock Doctrine: The Rise of Disaster Capitalism*, London: Allen Lane.

Laclau, E. (1993) 'Discourse', in R. Goodin and P. Pettit (eds) *A Companion to Contemporary Political Philosophy*, Oxford: Blackwell, pp 431–7.

Malpass, P. and Murie, A. (1999) *Housing Policy and Practice*, 5th edn, Basingstoke: Macmillan.

Mises, L. (1981) *Socialism: An Economic and Social Analysis*, Indianapolis, IN: Liberty Fund.

Muller, J. (1997) 'Introduction: What is conservative social and political thought?', in J. Muller (ed) *Conservatism: An Anthology of Social and Political Thought from David Hume to the Present*, Princeton, NJ: Princeton University Press, pp 3–31.

Narveson, J. (1988) *The Libertarian Idea*, Philadelphia, PA: Temple University Press.

Nozick, R. (1974) *Anarchy, State and Utopia*, Oxford: Blackwell.

Nozick, R. (2001) *Invariance: The Structure of the Objective World*, Cambridge, MA: Belknap/Harvard University Press.

Oakeshott, M. (1991) *Rationalism in Politics and Other Essays*, new and expanded edn, Indianapolis, IN: Liberty Press.

ODPM (Office of the Deputy Prime Minister) (2003) *Sustainable Communities: Building for the Future*, London: ODPM.

ODPM (2005) *Sustainable Communities: Homes for All: A Five Year Plan from the ODPM*, London: ODPM.

O'Hara, K. (2005) *After Blair: Conservatism Beyond Thatcher*, Cambridge: Icon.

Quinton, A. (1993) 'Conservatism', in R. Goodin and P. Pettit (eds) *A Companion to Contemporary Political Philosophy*, Oxford: Blackwell, pp 244–68.

Ramsden, J. (1998) *An Appetite for Power: A History of the Conservative Party since 1830*, London: Harper Collins.

Ronald, R. (2008) *The Ideology of Home Ownership: Homeownership Societies and the Role of Housing*, Basingstoke: Palgrave Macmillan.

Saunders, P. (1990) *A Nation of Home Owners*, London: Allen and Unwin.

Schmidtz, D. (1998) 'Taking responsibility', in D. Schmidtz and R. Goodin (1998) *Social Welfare and Individual Responsibility*, Cambridge: Cambridge University Press, pp 1–96.

Scruton, R. (2000) *England: An Elegy*, London: Chatto and Windus.

Scruton, R. (2001) *The Meaning of Conservatism*, 3rd edn, Basingstoke: Palgrave.

Searle, J. (1995) *The Construction of Social Reality*, London: Allen Lane.

Shiller, R. (2008) *The Sub-Prime Solution: How Today's Global Financial Crisis Happened and What to Do About It*, Princeton, NJ: Princeton University Press.

Sillars, R. (2007) 'The development of the Right to Buy and the sale of council houses', *Economic Affairs*, vol 27, no 1, pp 52–7.

Somerville, P. and Bengtsson, B. (2002) 'Constructionism, realism and housing theory', *Housing, Theory and Society*, vol 19, nos 3–4, pp 121–36.

Torfing, J. (1999) *New Theories of Discourse: Laclau, Mouffe and Zizek*, Oxford: Blackwell.

Turner, J. (1976) *Housing by People: Towards Autonomy in Building Environments*, London: Marion Boyars.

Voegelin, E. (2002) *Anamnesis: On the Theory of History and Politics*, Columbia, MO: University of Missouri Press.

Ward, C. (1985) *When We Build Again, Let's Have Housing That Works*, London: Pluto Press.

Wilcox, S. (1999) *Housing Finance Review, 1999/2000*, York: Joseph Rowntree Foundation.

Wilcox, S. (2008) *UK Housing Review, 2007/2008*, York: Chartered Institute of Housing/Council for Mortgage Lenders.

Williams, N. (2003) 'The Right to Buy in Britain', in T. O'Sullivan and K. Gibb (eds) *Housing Economics and Public Policy*, Oxford: Blackwell, pp 235–47.

Wittgenstein, L. (1958) *Philosophical Investigations*, Oxford: Blackwell.

Wolf, M. (2009) *Fixing Global Capitalism*, New Haven, CT: Yale University Press.

Zizek, S. (1999) *The Ticklish Subject: The Absent Centre of Political Ontology*, London: Verso.

Index